# NATURAL GARDENS

# NATURAL GARDENS

*Series Concept:* Robert J. Dolezal
*Encyclopedia Concept:* Barbara K. Dolezal
*Managing Editor:* Jill Fox
*Development Editor:* Sudha Putnam
*Encyclopedia Writer:* Jane Merryman
*Natural Gardening Consultant:* Judy Adler
*Photography Editor:* John M. Rickard
*Designer:* Jerry Simon
*Layout:* Rik Boyd
*Photoshop Artist:* Gerald A. Bates
*Horticulturist:* Peggy Henry
*Photo Stylist:* Peggy Henry
*Copy Editor:* Barbara Coster
*Proofreaders:* Jane Merryman, Ken DellaPenta
*Index:* Aubrey McClellan, ALTA Indexing

Copyright © 2001
Creative Publishing international, Inc.
5900 Green Oak Drive
Minnetonka, MN 55343
1-800-328-3895
All rights reserved
Printed in U.S.A. by Quebecor World
10 9 8 7 6 5 4 3 2 1

*President/CEO:* David D. Murphy
*Vice President/Editorial:* Patricia K. Jacobsen
*Vice President/Retail Sales & Marketing:* Richard M. Miller

Home Improvement/*Gardening*
*Executive Editor:* Bryan Trandem
*Editorial Director:* Jerri Farris
*Creative Director:* Tim Himsel

Created by: Dolezal & Associates,
in partnership with Creative Publishing international, Inc.,
in cooperation with Black & Decker.
**BLACK&DECKER**. is a trademark of the Black & Decker
Corporation and is used under license.

Library of Congress Cataloging-in-Publication Data

Coit, Laura
  Natural gardens : landscaping with designs inspired by nature /
Laura Coit ; photographer, John Rickard.
     p. cm. -- (Black & Decker outdoor home)
  ISBN 0-86573-463-1 (hardcover) -- ISBN 0-86573-464-X (softcover)
  1. Natural gardens. 2. Natural landscaping. I. Title. II. Series.
SB439 .C65 2000
635.9'51--dc21
                                                  00-048504

ISBN 0–86573–463–1 (hardcover)
ISBN 0–86573–464–x (softcover)

# PHOTOGRAPHY & ILLUSTRATION

## PRINCIPAL PHOTOGRAPHY

**JOHN M. RICKARD:** Cover photograph and pgs. *iv (upper mid, lower mid, & bot), v, vi, vii, viii,* 2, 4, 5 (top R), 6, 7, 8 (top R & inset), 9, 12 (top, center, & bot), 13, 14, 15, 16, 17, 18, 19, 20, 21, 22, 24 (bot L), 25, 26 (top R & inset), 27, 28, 29, 30, 31, 32, 34, 37 (steps 1-4), 38, 39, 40, 41, 42 (steps 1 & 5), 43, 44, 45, 46, 47, 48, 50 (bot L), 51, 52, 53, 54 (top L), 55, 56, 57, 58, 59, 60, 61, 63, 64, 65, 66, 67, 68, 69, 70, 72 (top R & bot L), 73, 74 (bot L), 75, 76 (mid L), 77, 80 (top & mid), 81 (top), 82, (top & bot), 84, 85 (bot), 86 (top), 87 (mid & bot), 88 (top), 89 (top), 90 (mid), 91 (top), 92 (mid), 93 (bot), 95 (top & bot), 96, 97, 99, 100 (top & mid), 101 (top), 102 (top), 103 (top & mid), 104 (mid), 105 (mid & bot), 110 (top & bot), 111 (top & mid), 112 (top), 113 (top & bot), 114 (bot), 115 (top).

## OTHER PHOTOGRAPHY AND ILLUSTRATION

**TIM BUTLER:** pgs. 87 (top), 88 (mid), 98 (top), 112 (bot), 113 (mid).

**KYLE CHESSER:** pgs. 72 (inset), 76 (top R & bot L).

**CAB COVAY:** pg. 80 (bot).

**DOUG DEALEY:** pgs. 3 (top R), 50 (top), 54 (bot L), 81 (mid & bot).

**ROBERT J. DOLEZAL:** pgs. 12 (lower mid), 24 (top R), 26 (bot L), 36, 37 (step 5), 62, 93 (top).

**REED ESTABROOK:** pg. 78.

**SAXON HOLT:** pgs. 90 (bot), 92 (bot), 106 (mid).

**IMAGEPOINT:** pgs. 42 (steps 2–4 & 6), 83, 88 (bot), 112 (mid).

**DONNA KRISCHAN:** pgs. *iv* (top), 5 (bot L).

**CHARLES NUCCI:** pg 114 (mid).

**JERRY PAVIA:** pgs. 8 (bot mid), 85 (top & mid), 86 (mid & bot), 89 (mid), 90 (top), 92 (top), 93 (mid), 94, 98 (mid), 101 (mid & bot), 102 (mid & bot), 103 (bot), 104 (top), 105 (top), 106 (top), 107, 108 (top & mid), 109, 110 (mid), 111 (bot), 114 (top).

**CHARLES SLAY:** pgs. 3 (bot L), 82 (mid), 89 (bot), 91(mid & bot), 95 (mid), 98 (bot), 100 (bot), 106 (bot), 108 (bot), 115 (bot).

**BRIAN TAYLOR:** pgs. 10, 12 (upper mid).

**YVONNE WILLIAMS:** pgs. 74 (top R), 104 (bot), 115 (mid).

## ILLUSTRATIONS: HILDEBRAND DESIGN

## ACKNOWLEDGEMENTS

The editors acknowledge with grateful appreciation the contribution to this book of Alden Lane Nursery, Livermore, California; Wedekinds Garden Center, Sonoma, California; and to the following individuals: Rodney Friedrich, Betsy Niles, and Janet Tiffany.

# NATURAL GARDENS

Author
**Laura Coit**

Photographer
**John M. Rickard**

Series Concept
**Robert J. Dolezal**

CREATIVE
PUBLISHING
international

Minnetonka, Minnesota

# CONTENTS

# INTRODUCTION

My personal connection with the landscape comes from childhood summers spent on a remote lake in the Adirondack mountains of upstate New York. There, I learned each tree, fern, and wildflower. The spirit of the land captured my heart forever. In each place I've lived since then I've tried to create a garden that strengthens my connection to the region by duplicating the natural landscape.

My experience is far from unique; the North American continent is full of distinctive landscapes, each different, each a particular expression of the wonder of nature. What these gardens have in common is the awe they inspire. Many of us seek to re-create nature's splendor, transforming our home landscape into a garden that evokes the same feeling of well-being we have when visiting natural settings.

"
*Happily may I walk.
May it be beautiful before
me. May it be beautiful
behind me. May it be
beautiful below me. May it
be beautiful above me. May
it be beautiful all around
me. In beauty it is finished.*
"

*NAVAJO PRAYER*

Few activities are as satisfying to the human spirit as gardening. Gardening connects us to the earth and teaches children respect for our environment. Increased environmental awareness has prompted many of us to garden in a "natural" style. Natural gardens create a setting that reflects the beauty of the regional landscape, support a diverse group of plants, and perform well in local conditions.

Whether using plants native to the area, or plants that simply thrive there, natural gardens are in harmony with their environment. They rely on plants that will flourish by design, instead of requiring constant care. Generally, they conserve resources and encourage visits by birds, bees, and butterflies. Natural gardens provide a chance to take in nature's miracles, right outside your door.

A quiet landscaping revolution is taking place, one natural garden at a time. Natural gardeners are establishing home landscapes to suit their environment, whatever and wherever it may be. I invite you to experience natural gardening and creating a landscape that will reflect both your personality and the unique character of your surroundings. You will find that the endless wonder of nature awaits you.

# Beautiful Natural Gardens

Invite nature into your home by designing your garden in a style to reflect the world around you

What a glorious feeling to be surrounded by nature! With a natural garden, you create a space that makes this experience part of your daily life, right in your own backyard.

The home garden evolved as an enclosure to prevent nature's encroachment. In times past, gardeners labored long and hard to tame nature. Today, natural areas are disappearing and we feel the threat of spreading urbanization. Instead of walling nature out, we seek to create gardens that invite nature in. This movement has come to be called natural gardening. Natural gardening has three approaches:

**Natural style:** Embracing existing conditions and regional characteristics, these gardens are designed to resemble naturally occurring sites, often nearby natural landscapes. These gardens are produced in regional themes, such as a meadow, woodland, desert, or marsh. They are casual and asymmetrical. Structures and accents also often use materials found in local surroundings, such as curved paths of local gravel or mulch, and borders of fieldstone. Natural style gardens fit more than country sites —they're perfect for the city and suburbs, too.

**Native plant gardening:** Use only plants native to the region to create a garden where plants thrive, are beautiful within the setting, and are easy to maintain. Often these gardens become havens for attracting local birds and butterflies. Create natural gardens with native plants or with plants well-adapted to the soil conditions and climate.

**Environmentally friendly:** These gardens are maintained using organic methods rather than synthetic fertilizers and pesticides. Choose appropriate plants, improve the soil, and learn about pests, diseases, and their natural remedies in order to create a pesticide-free garden that is healthy for birds, butterflies, children, and pets. Any style garden can be maintained this way, whether it's natural in style, uses native plants, or is a traditional landscape.

*The more you learn about your natural environment, the better suited your garden will be to its surroundings.*

## LEARNING FROM NATURE

Learn from nature by being open to its inspiration. Nature can be both bold and subtle. It awes with breathtaking beauty and invites quiet reflection of its ways.

Seek nature's lessons everywhere, perhaps right out your window or across the street. Investigate, as you pass in your car each day, any forests, meadows, or wetlands. Travel to a nearby park, public garden, nature preserve, or the countryside in search of inspiration.

Through observation, you'll discover the spirit of the land. Look carefully at landforms, habitat, rocks, soil, and especially plants. See how scenes change with the seasons. Observe plant combinations and colors. Look at the wild-flowers—often natives—thriving with little care. Plants related to these wildflowers will need little care to flourish.

Challenge yourself to think about gardening in new ways. Consider how to create a garden that stimulates your imagination, reflects lessons found in your observations, and echoes natural surroundings—urban, suburban, or rural.

Capture that which is unique to your home. Are there plants whose form or flowers define your region? Do geographic features set the tone? Are there places with which you connect emotionally? Are there plants that delight you each season? Natural garden themes vary by region just as our favorite foods and regional accents vary. A cottage garden in New England is very different from one in British Columbia. A Minnesota wetland is distinct from one hugging Oregon's coast. Regional character, climatic conditions, special plants, and unique people fuse to make each garden distinct.

*(Top) Choose materials that blend garden features into the natural surroundings. Here, a bench has been carved gracefully from a fallen tree. Its natural color and texture fit its setting.*

*(Bottom) Naturalized daffodils turn a meadow into a sea of gold in early spring.*

The cottage garden mimics nature's boisterous abundance. It includes trees, shrubs, perennials, and herbs. This bounty contrasts markedly with the standard urban landscape of turfgrass and shrubs. In the cottage garden, flowers and foliage mingle with casual profusion. Its romantic style can work equally well in the city, suburbs, or countryside.

**ROMANTIC COTTAGE GARDENS**

The trick to creating a successful cottage garden is to use plants that thrive in your conditions—a key tenet of the natural garden. Native plants echo the original, uncultivated landscape and visually link the garden to its surrounding environmental region.

Forget about the quaint, thatched-roof cottage when creating a cottage garden. Any modest-sized dwelling and the right approach fills the bill. Most cottage gardens are in enclosed front areas, often with a gate and a walkway to the front door of the home. Flowering plants abound inside the enclosure. Native plants, local building materials, and whimsical decorations tie the garden to its location.

The cottage garden theme is as amenable to homes in the west as it is to the east. These gardens, however, will look vastly different. A southwestern cottage garden can contain prickly pear, Adam's-needle, and drifts of drought-tolerant flowers against adobe walls. A cottage garden in a mid-Atlantic state might feature native dogwood and false indigo mixed with well-adapted nonnatives, including Siberian iris and ornamental onions. Wherever you live, a cottage garden offers unlimited opportunity for experimentation and enjoyment.

*(Top) A natural garden provides abundant opportunity for every child to see and appreciate their environment in the company of a trusted adult.*

*(Bottom) A mixed planting with a variety of flowers creates an exuberant display. Blurred lines between plants is a key feature of a natural cottage garden.*

## WOODLAND BOWERS

The beauty found in a mature deciduous forest is sublime. In these woodlands, the forest floor comes into bloom before the overstory trees leaf out in late spring. Then the high canopy provides a sheltering umbrella for the lush understory growth of shrubs, small trees, ferns, moss, and wildflowers.

As a theme, woodland gardens take many guises. Generally, woodlands boast a mixture of trees, rich soils, and often plenty of rainfall. To give your woodland bower a local flair, study the natural forest in your region. Much of the eastern half of North America was once covered with just such a forest. Fortunately, fragments remain for your observation. Other regions also possess forested areas, from the temperate rain forest of British Columbia, to the high mountain forests of the Rockies, to the oak savannas of California. Let these peaceful forests inspire you to create a restful retreat of your own.

*(Top) Much of the beauty of the woodland garden comes from foliage texture such as the plantain lily and fern seen here.*

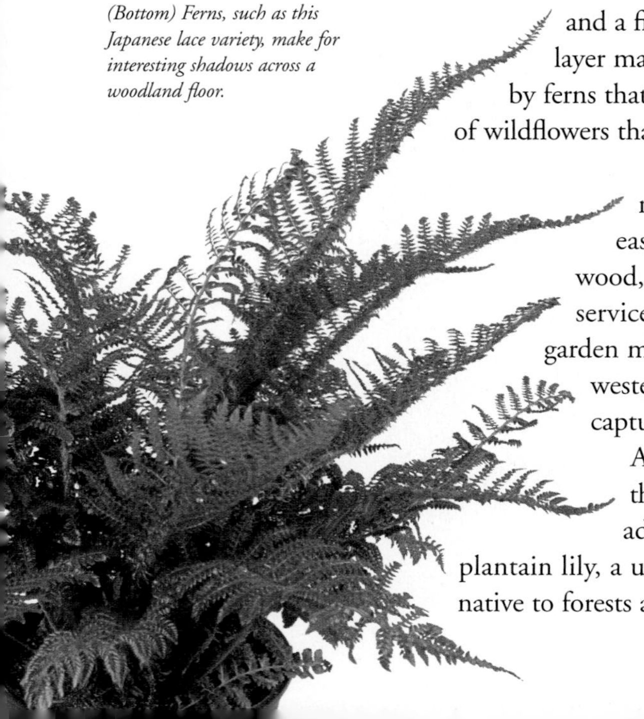

*(Bottom) Ferns, such as this Japanese lace variety, make for interesting shadows across a woodland floor.*

Woodland gardens are characterized by their dappled, tree-cast shade. Plants are arranged in layers: an overstory of tall trees, an understory of small trees and medium-height shrubs, and a final floor level of perennials and ground covers. The overstory layer may be accented with vines and the understory layer enhanced by ferns that add a graceful character. Many woodland floors boast drifts of wildflowers that bloom before trees leaf.

Though all woodland gardens may look similar, the regional plants that create the effect are different. A southeastern woodland garden might contain native azaleas, dogwood, plantain lilies, and ferns; a northeastern garden might host serviceberry, redbud, and wake-robin; and a Pacific northwestern garden might show off wild ginger, Oregon grape, wood sorrel, and western sword fern. All echo the native woods in an attempt to capture their magic.

Also consider plants that are native to other woodlands around the world. When their growing conditions are met, many plants adapt well to woodland gardens in other areas. Note that the plantain lily, a ubiquitous resident of the North American shade garden, is native to forests and shady stream banks of Japan.

Meadows—sunny openings between forest areas—bring to mind visions of sun and flowers. Meadows are increasingly common as agricultural land is left fallow. Meadow-inspired wildflower gardens and perennial beds replicate the carefree beauty of these open spaces.

The midwest was once home to a massive ocean of grassland called prairie. This undulating land contained a rich mixture of grasses and wildflowers. The stirring beauty of this unique North American habitat is restored in prairie gardens.

The inspiration of meadow and prairie has led to an innovative theme called the New American Garden, where free-spirited ornamental grasses are artfully arranged with drifts of perennials and bulbs. Suggestive of the prairie, these gardens may contain native prairie plants, as well as others matched to local growing conditions.

Prairie grasses and flowers are a natural fit for the Great Plains and other areas with dry summers and cold winters. The prairie garden restores the natural balance to the land, preventing soil erosion, avoiding garden chemical and pesticide use, reducing watering, and welcoming native songbirds and butterflies.

You may choose to turn your front yard into a prairie "lawn," plant a wildflower meadow in your backyard, or simply incorporate prairie plants into a naturalistic perennial bed. Many resident plants of the prairie are welcome migrants to urban or suburban gardens. Some of the most popular and colorful garden perennials are native to the grasslands, including purple coneflower and black-eyed Susans.

To create a prairie garden, plant flowers and grasses together, select plants that complement each other, and choose plants well adapted to your climate and soil. Meadow gardens take some special care, including an annual mowing and weed control, but the results are breathtaking.

## MEADOW AND PRAIRIE INSPIRATIONS

*(Inset) Create a meadow in place of a typical turfgrass lawn with a lively mix of wildflowers, here a packaged mix of annual and perennial species.*

*(Bottom) Butterflies find colorful purple coneflowers an enticing garden addition.*

## COAST AND SEASIDE

*(Inset) Ground covers serve a purpose in erosion prevention in an area of moving sand dunes.*

*(Bottom) Tall plants function as a means to break the prevailing onshore sea winds that blow in many coast locations.*

Ocean breezes and panoramic views draw people to the coasts. The spectacular views that accompany a seaside garden come with conditions that help create dramatic beauty: sandy or rocky soil, dunes or craggy shoreline, and exposure to salt-laden winds and sea spray.

The coast and seaside theme varies from the rocky shores of Newfoundland to the sandy beaches of the Gulf of Mexico. The weather varies as well, from the ocean-influenced "Mediterranean" climate of Oregon and California to the hot summers and cool, wet winters of Washington and British Columbia. Your garden design should reflect the geography. A wide stretch of Atlantic beachfront may benefit from paths interspersed with dune grasses, while steep Pacific frontage could be terraced and planted with the varied textures of evergreen, drought-tolerant shrubs.

Coast gardens, in all their variety, generally benefit from the moderating effect of the ocean. As in other natural garden themes, the site dictates the plantings. To thrive in seaside locations, plants must tolerate sandy or rocky soil, the natural rainfall patterns, possibly salt spray, and often a strong prevailing wind. Study the native and naturalized plants found in your area to discover the tough ones that can tolerate the challenging conditions.

Native grasses and salt-tolerant shrubs can stabilize soil, preventing erosion. Installing a windbreak near your dwelling could help create a usable microclimate.

## DESERT AND ARID GARDENS

Seeing the desert in bloom is a yearly phenomenon always remembered by those lucky enough to witness it. By definition, the only requirement for a "desert" is that it have scant precipitation, which means that parts of the Antarctic actually are polar desert. For gardening purposes, deserts are characterized by poor sandy soils, low rainfall, and extreme temperatures. Arid landscapes receive more rain than do deserts, but still less than 20 inches (50 cm) a year.

Desert and arid gardens often are referred to as xeriscape landscaping. A xeriscape is a landscape that requires minimal irrigation and incorporates a few important principles that can be applied to any area. Only plants well adapted to the area are planted, plants with similar water needs are grouped together, any water is applied efficiently, and the area devoted to water-thirsty turf is reduced. Each principle is important in desert and arid locations.

An amazing array of plants has developed strategies to prosper through the drought, searing heat, and sudden downpours in brief rainy seasons that typify desert and arid regions. Desert and arid gardens combine succulents, cacti, and other plants well adapted to harsh conditions. Annuals and perennials add to the riot of spring color. Deep-rooted trees, walled courtyards, and shade structures provide some protection from the sun. Good drainage prevents standing water and runoff during periods of rain. The desert garden can be an oasis of color and texture that integrates your home into a distinctive landscape evocative of the natural desert habitat.

*(Top) Massing cacti around landscape rocks presents an interesting combination of textures in an arid setting.*

*(Inset) A major goal when designing sparse desert landscapes is to soften and blend the edge between the landscaped area and its natural surroundings.*

## STREAMS AND WETLANDS

Humans are drawn to water in all its forms, wherever it exists. Water coolly transforms a garden: calm water is serene and restful, while rushing water is lively and exciting. A water feature adds a special element to any garden and creates new planting opportunities.

Our natural streams and wetlands—bogs, marshes, and swamps—are a precious resource. These unique areas host a wide range of specialized plants, are sites of important environmental functions, and support abundant wildlife. Stream and wetland gardens can incorporate existing streams, ponds, and marshy areas, or they can be created especially to mimic a natural setting. If you are fortunate enough to have a natural wetland as part of your site, approach your gardening efforts with environmental awareness and sensibilities.

It's fairly simple to construct a natural-looking pond, pool, or stream. A bog garden can be a great solution to an area where water stands. Moisture-loving plants might thrive in this area where little previously would grow. A stream garden, waterfall, pond, or pool can be created where a natural spring already exists, or a water feature can be fabricated from scratch, using a recirculating pump and specialized liners readily available at many home and garden stores.

A pool or pond creates an opportunity for specialized plants. Submerged aquatics and moisture-loving shoreline plants flourish in and around water features, providing a rich habitat for wildlife.

Choose an appropriate location when planning a spontaneous-looking water feature. A low spot or depression is the ideal place for a pond. Use local materials to blend the feature's edges into the landscape. Stone is a natural complement to water. Integrate a water feature with the rest of your garden by plantings on its shoreline.

Water—natural or installed—adds immeasurably to a home landscape. Consider a fern-filled glade with a rushing stream, a contemplative pool, or a flat, serene pond with lush, vertical plants. These memorable garden pictures are possible in nearly any region.

*Native trees can provide a visual bridge between the planted landscape found near a home and natural plantings along a nearby stream.*

*A whimsical metal and concrete bridge spans a small pond alive with iris and arrowhead.*

Who can resist a tropical paradise? The tropical garden is an exuberant jungle, full of lush green vegetation, colorful foliage, and bright, exotic flowers. In this warm, humid climate with plenty of rainfall, plants grow rapidly and abundantly. The shape, texture, and form of luxurious foliage are the dominant elements. The tropical garden blurs the boundary between exotic wildness and cultivation.

## TROPICAL GARDENS

A garden with a tropical theme mimics the natural tropical forest understory. Look to parks and public gardens for inspiration. Consider the wide range of plants native to tropical zones that produce luxuriant and colorful foliage. Use vines to lend a jungle feel. Choose plants considered exotic elsewhere, including bird-of-paradise, philodendron, and ti plant. The very names bring to mind a tropical dreamland.

Because of their strong vertical and textural attributes, tropical plants can have a great impact in your garden, even those situated in small spaces. Just one or two large tropical plants can establish a luxurious look to be enjoyed throughout the year. Consider protected, warm, windfree locations when creating gardens featuring tropical plants.

Designing with tropical plants in locations outside the tropical climate zones is a gardening style called Tropicalismo. These striking gardens work particularly well in areas where the native landscape already is lush in its appearance or in sites isolated from any genuine natural landscape. Tropicalismo is prevalent in the U.S. coastal Pacific northwest and in Canada's coastal

British Columbia, where a wide range of hardy tropical-looking plants can be grown outdoors with occasional protection from cool temperatures during the winter.

If you have a city balcony, a tropical container garden creates a little bit of paradise in Tropicalismo style for the summer months. Place the containers in a sheltered, sunny location and provide regular mistings of water to keep the plants hydrated and happy. Remember that tropicals need high fertility, oftentimes with acidic soil conditions.

*(Top) Lush plantings and bright accents such as this amaryllis are typical of the showy displays seen in many tropical gardens.*

*(Bottom) When your site and climate are suitable, even small spaces adapt well to tropical themes and plants.*

**As tempting as it may be to start planting, successful gardens begin with time spent considering all your options**

# A Garden Checklist

Once you've decided to design, build, and plant a natural garden, streamline your garden-making process by thinking through exactly what you want from the garden before you get out and start digging in the soil. Using nature as your inspiration, get ready to make some practical decisions.

This chapter presents information on making the best choices for your garden by determining its purpose, knowing the type of plants your site and soil will support, and understanding how everything you want will fit into the available space on your landscape site. You will understand the necessary skills, tools, and materials you'll need to install a natural garden, and you'll discover the available sources for plants and more information.

Inspired by the multitude of garden themes found throughout North America, now it's time for you to narrow your choice of garden themes to the one's that fit your home and your region [see Beautiful Natural Gardens, pg. 1]. Some natural garden themes—cottage, woodland, and coastal—can be adapted to many regions. Others—desert and tropical—are more region specific.

Also consider both your time and resources as you narrow your garden design choices. A natural garden inspired by a meadow or prairie can be created simply—in some cases from seed—and established in a single season. If plants are chosen that suit your area's natural precipitation, they can thrive for years with little upkeep beyond seasonal care. The installation of a stream or wetland garden, on the other hand, involves planning and building structural features and careful attention to upkeep.

The same natural garden design guidelines apply regardless of the garden theme you choose. Those guidelines, which are presented on the following pages, begin with an understanding of the environment found around you.

*Arranging new garden features and plants around existing plants is an important aspect of natural gardening. This house and deck were designed to coordinate with the stunning hundred-year-old cactus on the hillside.*

## MATCH NATURAL SURROUNDINGS

Choosing plants that will complement your garden theme and thrive in your garden is an important part of planning your garden. To help you determine the type of plants that will grow in your garden, you'll need to know the plant hardiness zone where you live. The United States Department of Agriculture [USDA] has developed a map that divides all of North America and other areas of the world into eleven regions based on the average coldest temperature [see USDA Plant Hardiness Around the World, pg. 116]. In addition to your hardiness zone, gain an understanding of your region's general climate and the microclimate influences of your garden site and around your home before choosing your plants.

Begin by studying your climate. Understand how the general climate in your region affects your landscape. Consider annual rainfall, how sun and shade patterns change throughout the seasons, and prevailing winds. Also consider the topography of your landscape and any microclimates on your site where conditions vary from the norm. A good example is the south-facing wall of a home, which generally is warmer and sunnier than its north-facing wall.

*(Above) Meadows fill with wildflowers in springtime. Natural gardens mimic them with massed displays of bloom.*

*(Right) Blend arid gardens from nature to landscape by selecting similar materials and plants.*

One goal of a natural garden is that it blend in: with your home, with the natural surroundings, and also with your community. Study your surroundings, including local architecture, geological features, and cultural customs. Consider the color, style, and size of your home as well as those homes and yards around you. Research any local ordinances, zoning, covenants, or other regulations that could impact your project. If you have nearby neighbors, share your plans with them.

*(Above) Include seating areas to enjoy your garden's vistas.*

*(Right) A rain forest is a dim and damp environment.*

*(Bottom) Observe nature's trends as you choose your plants.*

Try to find out the original condition of your land. Was it a forest, desert, prairie, or meadow? Does any such habitat still exist? Are there nearby physical features—lakes, mountains, ocean, or wetlands—that set the tone for your site? Can you borrow views—or landscaping ideas—from adjacent natural areas?

As you explore the natural habitat around you, become familiar with native and naturalized plants that thrive there. Such plants are adapted to life in your climate and most likely will fit your garden theme. Note the type of plants and also their arrangement. The layered planting pattern of a woodland, for example, is very different from the sparse planting pattern in a desert. Mimicking plants and planting patterns helps link your garden to its native environment.

Another method to employ to give your garden a sense of belonging to its region is incorporating local building and landscaping materials. Using local materials both reflects your community's unique character and usually helps keep the project within your budget.

An important step in creating your garden is determining its purpose and function. Forming a clear understanding of why you're choosing a natural garden and how your garden will be used makes all your design, material, and plant choices easier.

## PURPOSE AND FUNCTION

As you're considering a natural garden, you'll want to create a beautiful space in harmony with its natural surroundings. Under this umbrella, the possibilities are endless. It's important to delve deeper for more precise motives.

Ask yourself the specific reasons you have for creating your new natural garden: Perhaps you want to control water consumption by reducing the amount of water-guzzling lawn. Maybe you want to beautify a shady urban backyard so you can enjoy the view from inside. On the other hand, you might desire to attract more birds to your yard. Maybe you want to create an entry garden that lends a welcoming appearance to your home. Perhaps there is a neighbor's garage to screen from view or a hard-to-mow slope. Maybe you're looking for a garden where your children can learn about nature and the environmentally sound way to garden. Finally, you may just love gardening and want to increase the diversity of plants in your yard. Each of these ideas—and millions more—can be used to define a garden's purpose.

Reflect on how your garden will function: understand who will use it and their requirements. Think about your needs for privacy and desire to share your garden space. Perhaps you need a place where children can play, a retreat for entertaining, or a quiet spot for relaxing. Consider how the garden will be viewed, both from inside the house and from the outdoor living areas. Contemplate the times of day and seasons of the year when you want to use your garden. Each of these ideas can affect the function of your garden, its size, and its placement.

Think about the purpose and function of your garden as time passes. As your family grows, its needs will change. A children's play area today may be a fine location for a more contemplative patio area or water garden in a few years. Plants, too, take time to mature. If creating a windbreak is an important part of your garden's function, install a temporary screen to serve that purpose now, and plant a row of shrubs that will grow in a few years into a natural windbreak. As the shrubs mature, you'll be able to remove the screen and complete the garden.

While you're contemplating the garden's purpose and function, also think about how much care you can provide. Consider its need for watering, mulching, pruning, and cleanup. Plan a garden within limits that you can maintain by yourself, unless you'll be using helpers to assist you. Automated systems, such as in-ground irrgation on a timer, save countless hours and assures your garden regular watering.

*Creating privacy while reducing noise were prime considerations for the design of this attractive garden landscape. The brick wall deadens street noise, yet is a good fit with the home's brick facade. The plantings ensure that traffic into the yard will be blocked, yet remain attractive and inviting to passersby.*

## ANALYZE THE SITE

Take a matter-of-fact look at the conditions in your yard—this is vital to effective design and long-term plant health. Measure your site and decide on the area or areas that you want to make into your natural garden. Consider the climate and any microclimates, as well as the seasonal sun, shade, and wind conditions that surround your home [see Match Natural Surroundings, pg. 12].

*When in doubt, use a compass to determine your garden's facing. Remember that sunlight is greatest in sites exposed to the south, while eastern and western exposures usually have partial sun conditions.*

Catalog your site's existing features. Look at all the physical elements such as buildings and other structures, fences, paths, patios, and large rocks. Determine the features that suit your new garden purpose and function and those that match your natural garden theme. Think how these features can be adapted or remodeled to suit your new look.

Check the grade or slope of the land. Look for signs of erosion or standing water. Consider different ways to utilize a steep slope [see Grades and Elevations, pg. 36].

Determine the location of utility lines, including gas, electric, water, sewer, telephone, and cable. Consider how their location might affect your new garden. Check any land-use restrictions concerning landscaping over utility lines. You also want to know where the lines are located that you want to utilize. If one purpose of your new garden is to lessen maintenance chores through the addition of an irrigation system, access to water lines is essential. If a function of your new garden is night safety, access to electric lines for lighting will be important.

Consider drainage around your home. Making major landscaping changes can alter irrigation and rainwater flow. A landscaping project can be an opportunity to ensure that areas that have poor drainage are corrected. Always make changes with caution to avoid causing water to flow into your home or your neighbor's yard [see Drainage, Irrigation, and Lighting, pg. 40].

*A northern exposure, even in warm-winter climates, is a fitting environment for shade plants that will tolerate morning and evening sunlight. Here, plantain lily, geranium, and astilbe are planted close to the house, where shade is most dense.*

Examine all existing plants—trees, shrubs, perennials, and flowers—to determine if they are healthy and whether they will fit into your natural garden style [see Encyclopedia of Natural Garden Plants, pg. 79].

## UNDERSTAND THE SOIL

While one of the goals of a natural garden is to install plants that thrive under existing conditions, your soil may have been altered from its native state by past use: construction, agriculture, or prior gardening practices. Understanding your soil will help you in choosing plants and determining if your soil needs amendment with organic materials prior to planting.

Soil is a mix of various mineral particles, organic matter, air, and water. The mineral particles generally are sand, silt, or clay. A roughly equal mixture of all three is called loam. Organic matter is the decaying remains of once-living vegetable and animal matter. All soil contains organic matter in varying amounts. Organic matter influences the fertility and structure of the soil.

Different plants thrive in different types of soil. Because there's little you can do to change your soil's mineral content, choose plants that grow well in soil of that type: Sandy soil has large particles, drains quickly, traps more air, is prone to drought, and lacks water-soluble nutrients. Clay soil has smaller particles, drains more slowly, may become deficient in oxygen, but is moist and fertile. Loam holds both water and air, releasing them slowly for absorption by a plant's roots.

The most desirable soil for gardening generally is well-drained loam. You can improve the texture and increase fertility and benefical soil organisms of your soil through the addition of soil amendments, including compost [see Amending the Soil, pg. 47]. The key to growing plants successfully, however, is to create a close fit between your soil type and the plants' need. Many natural gardens succeed, more due to their judicious plant choices than because they have naturally rich or amended soil.

Another important factor of your soil is its pH, the measure of its degree of acidity or alkalinity. The pH scale ranges from 0–14—highly acidic to very alkaline—with 7.0 as neutral. Most plants do well from about 6.0–7.5 pH. Acidity or alkalinity is determined by the rock where the soil originated, precipitation, and the type of vegetation previously grown in the soil. When soils are either very acid or very alkaline, specific mineral elements important to plant growth become bound in the soil rather than being available for absorption by the plant. When the plant becomes deficient in an essential mineral, it weakens and becomes more susceptible to pests and diseases. Of course, some plants thrive in more acidic or more alkaline soils because they do not require the mineral that is blocked.

If you are unfamiliar with the type or pH of the soil in your yard, use a home soil test kit available from nurseries and garden centers. For more detailed information, send a soil sample to a testing lab recommended by your garden retailer, the USDA Cooperative Extension Service, or Agriculture Canada.

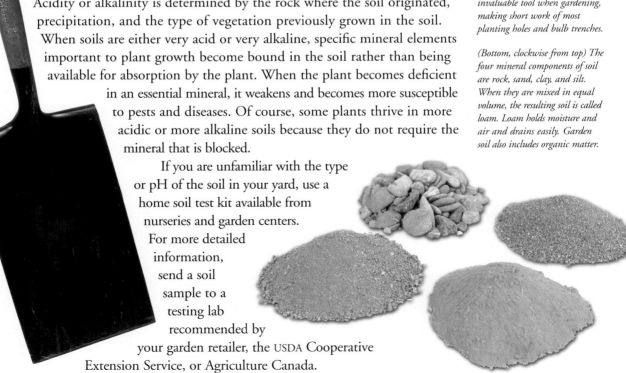

*(Left) A sharp spade is an invaluable tool when gardening, making short work of most planting holes and bulb trenches.*

*(Bottom, clockwise from top) The four mineral components of soil are rock, sand, clay, and silt. When they are mixed in equal volume, the resulting soil is called loam. Loam holds moisture and air and drains easily. Garden soil also includes organic matter.*

## PLAN MODIFICATIONS

*(Inset) A natural-appearing stream already may exist on the site or, as here, result from installing a recirculating pump and liner.*

*(Bottom) Walls can be used to terrace hillsides or make elevation changes on flat sites. Most natural gardens call for the use of local stone.*

Ask yourself these important questions: What modifications are necessary for my garden to perform its function? How can my garden serve its intended purpose?

Look carefully at the features recorded in your site analysis. How can they help or hinder? Determine how to accentuate positive features. Plant woodland gardens under existing shade trees, for example, or remove hedges to expose a gorgeous view.

Think creatively. Sloping sites with a steep grade can erode and be difficult to maintain. The site could be terraced, forming level planting beds with attractive steps; groundcover could be planted to hold the soil and eliminate mowing; or the steep grade could provide a course for a rushing stream or waterfall garden [see Grades and Elevations, pg. 36]. Consider your options as you plan site modifications.

Think of outdoor rooms—patios, decks, and eating areas—taking into account the views, both to and from the space. Consider microclimates—a patio with a northern exposure is cooler, while southern exposures offer warmth and sunshine. If nighttime use is planned, will you install 12-volt lighting?

Evaluate care needs and decide if you'll save watering time by installing an irrigation system or make other changes to the landscape.

As you plan modifications, look for ways to coordinate features with your theme. Paths, for example, make your garden accessible and also set a visual tone. They are an excellent means to introduce indigenous stone or other regional materials to your garden.

Finally, consider your resources. Estimate the effort and budget required for your site modifications, materials, and plants. The answers to these questions affect your decisions and how you phase the project.

Now's the time for some self-analysis. Assess your skills and the spirit you bring to your project. Also look to your toolshed for necessary equipment.

Think about the project's scope. Are you adding a few beds or planning a major overhaul? Does your schedule account for delays caused by the onset of inclement weather? Honestly appraise your time, interest, and physical abilities. If your project is large or strains your confidence, consider seeking a landscape architect, designer, or installation contractor. Choose potential candidates knowledgeable about the natural garden concept.

Identify local sources for regional building materials. Visit landscape supply outlets, nurseries, garden centers, and quarries to determine the availability of mulches, stone, soil amendments, and other needs.

Gardening requires some basic tools, and installing a landscape may require some specialized equipment. Landscaping equipment is often available at rental yards. The right tool for the job can make all the difference. You'll need trowels, round point shovels, a sharp square-bladed spade, a steel garden rake, a leaf rake, a spading fork, and sharp bypass pruners. You'll also need a wheelbarrow or garden cart to transport plants and materials. For pruning trees and large shrubs, add a pruning saw and long-handled loppers.

For watering, you'll need several lengths of hose, a watering wand with a diffusing rose, and a watering can.

If your garden is expansive, consider a small tiller for help with bed preparation and a leaf shredder for mulching leaves and twigs. To help amend your soil with compost, consider compost bins.

On the personal side, choose tools that are sized right for you. Border spades are much easier to use than are heavy nursery spades. Remember sturdy gloves, a brimmed hat, and rugged, waterproof boots to make your gardening safer and easier.

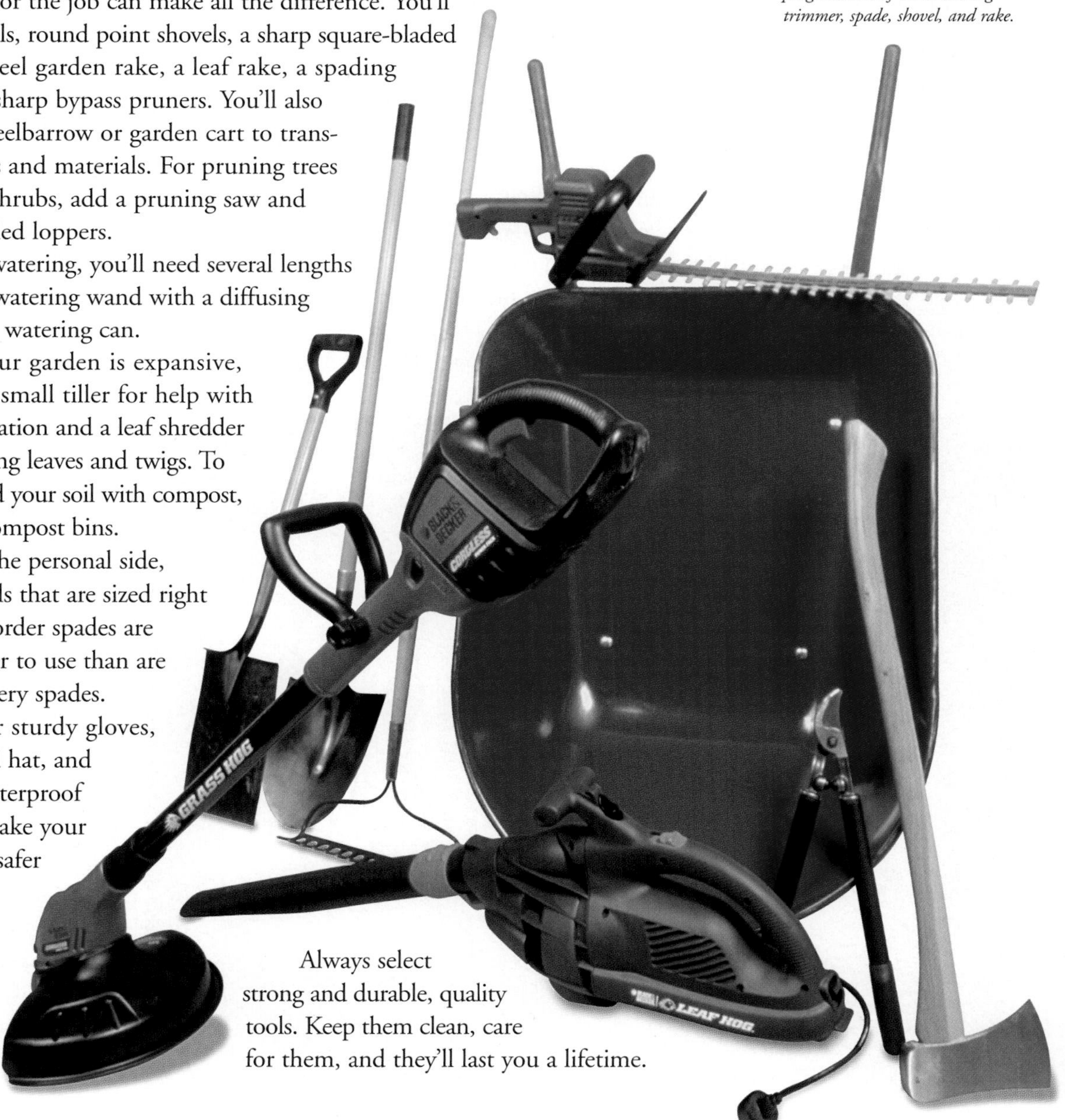

# SKILLS, TOOLS, AND MATERIALS

*(Bottom, clockwise from top) Natural gardens require reduced care as compared to traditional home landscapes. Still, tools and equipment are necessary for digging, raking, pruning, and maintenance. Pictured below are the large tools most commonly used in a natural garden: hedge trimmer, wheelbarrow, axe, lopping shears, leaf blower, string trimmer, spade, shovel, and rake.*

Always select strong and durable, quality tools. Keep them clean, care for them, and they'll last you a lifetime.

## CONSIDER AND SELECT PLANTS

Although it's too soon to begin digging holes, it's a perfect time to consider the plants you're going to include in your natural garden. You'll need to make a decision about the natural garden approach you want to take concerning plants. One approach is to select only native plants. Another is to include natives as well as selected plants that are native elsewhere but well-adapted to growing in your region.

First, make a list of all your favorites. Are there plants so special to you or to your location that you just have to find them a place in your natural garden? Perhaps as an American southeasterner you've always dreamed of flowering dogwoods, as a westerner longed for an orange drift of California poppy, or as a Vancouver Islander pictured a landscape filled with azaleas. Next, consider those plants in your natural surroundings. Which combine well and seem to flourish with little special care?

Confirm your USDA plant hardiness zone, and keep in mind your climate, microclimates—sun, shade, wind—and soil type [see USDA Plant Hardiness Zones Around the World, pg. 116]. Choose plants that are well matched to your site and garden theme to help ensure success as well as reduce necessary care.

Consult the photographs and descriptions found in this book [see Encyclopedia of Natural Garden Plants, pg. 79] to find many plants that grow well throughout North America. Each plant listing includes helpful planting tips, soil needs, hardiness zone, habit, design ideas, and garden theme suggestions.

Finally, think like a designer. Do you expect your plants to perform specific functions? Do you need a plant for a screen or an overhead canopy? Is there a steep slope to anchor with ground cover? Gather ideas now, and when the time comes you'll be ready to fill your plant list [see Creating a Planting Planner, pg. 33].

*The choice of natural garden plants spans cultivated and native plants, bulbs, annuals, perennials, shrubs, and trees— both evergreen and deciduous. Start your search at a garden center that specializes in native and natural garden plants, using your plant hardiness zone and climate as important criteria.*

*Visit arboretums, public gardens, and nearby parks to gain insight into the plant communities that are found in your area. Read informational brochures and guides for clues about unusual plants that you can showcase in your natural landscape.*

You'll have an abundance of assistance and wisdom if you consult others as you plan your natural garden. Start by investigating local sources of information.

Find a reliable nursery or garden center that stocks a range of plants suited to your region, plus tools and materials. Ask advice from staff on the "nuts and bolts" of installing and planting a new garden and listen to their plant recommendations. Look for employees who understand local conditions and have plenty of first-hand knowledge. If you are interested in a specific type of plant—native or aquatic, for example—seek out specialty nurseries. These retailers often have staff especially trained in the installation and care of their specialty.

## OBTAINING ADVICE

Start your search for information and advice at a nursery or garden center with experienced, knowledgeable staff. Give some thought to your objectives—the purpose of your garden, theme, and function along with your specific site conditions—before asking for options.

Electronic sources also have information and advice about plants and gardening practices from every part of the world.

Local libraries, public gardens, cooperative extension services, and universities also are good advice and information sources.

Before selecting specific plants, visit your local retailer—it's an excellent opportunity to become familiar with the range of plants and the sizes that are available to you. Cultivate a good relationship with a retailer and you'll always have someone to whom to turn for advice.

Seek out displays of natural gardens. Native preserves, botanical gardens, local parks, historic homes, and zoos—even many malls and business parks—employ gardeners who design and install natural gardens. Observe and ask questions whenever possible. Stop and talk to homeowners with gardens that capture your attention. Most gardeners welcome a chance to talk plants.

Take a gardening class at your local adult education program to learn about gardening and meet like-minded people. Many public gardens, community colleges, adult education centers, and park groups offer

a range of learning opportunities—from examples of regional gardening themes, to labeled plant collections and horticultural classes or lectures.

Look for local gardening clubs and native plant societies. Often, these organizations sponsor events where gardeners get together to share information, camaraderie, and plants.

If you live in an isolated or rural area, consider direct sources for hard-to-find plants. Specialty nurseries have a wide range of greengoods ready for delivery to your front door. Often their catalogs provide a wealth of descriptive information, and staff can be reached over the telephone or electronically to answer your questions. Many electronic retailers post photographs and detailed information about plants, along with helpful advice on their culture.

*Use electronic sources to find information about natural gardens, native plants, and gardening techniques [see On-line, pg. 118]. You can learn a great deal from the experience and research of others in forums and chat rooms. Remember to modify any advice to your locale.*

## NATURAL GARDEN PLANNING FLOWCHART

$A$ flowchart is a written checklist that allows you to quickly scan the major decisions that should be made as you consider your natural garden project. The one illustrated here is designed as a specific checklist for planning a natural garden. Use this flowchart to save time and effort, including second trips to the nursery or garden center.

**1** **Site Choice Questions:**
Where is your garden located, both geographically and within your yard? Is your proposed garden next to your home or another structure? If so, do you want to accentuate or downplay the style or color of the structure? Are there existing features or plants that should be incorporated or removed? What is your elevation? Is the site exposed to prevailing winds? Is it near an ocean or other body of water? Is your site level or does it slope?

## DETERMINING YOUR OBJECTIVES

**2** **Goal Questions:**
What approach to natural gardening will you take? Will you plant only natives? Is your gardening environmentally friendly? What theme best suits you? What purpose do you want your garden to serve? What are the functions you hope to gain from this garden? When do you need or want the project finished? How much ongoing care can you provide the garden?

## PLANNING FOR THE PROJECT

## ALLOCATING TIME AND SCHEDULE

**3** **Scale Questions:**
Is your space wandering and wide, or small and compact? Do you want to accentuate or minimize the dimensions of your site? Do you have the equipment needed to install and maintain this size garden? Can you find locally all the materials? How and when they can be delivered? How much time will building this project and installing the plants take? Will you need professional services or help in order to complete this project successfully? Does this project adhere to local codes? Will you need a permit for construction?

**4** **Plant Selection Questions:** What are the growth habits, seasonal display, and care needs of the plants you desire? Does your planned space provide for those requirements? Have you identified your USDA plant hardiness zone? Does the site receive partial sun and, if so, is it in early morning, midday, or late afternoon? Have you familiarized yourself with common garden pests and diseases, and what preventive measures you should take while making your plant selection? Are the plants in the garden center or nursery well maintained, healthy, and free of pests? Is the staff knowledgeable and helpful?

## PREPARING TO PURCHASE PLANTS

## SOIL PREPARATION, MATERIALS, AND TOOLS

**5** **Preparation Questions:** What is the quality of your soil? Is it sandy, hard and compacted clay, or something in between? Does it drain too quickly and stay very dry most of the time, or does it drain slowly and retain puddles? Do you know your soil's pH level? Have you located all the tools and equipment you'll need for installation and maintenance? Have you located a good local source of building supplies and finishing materials? Will your site require modification? Are you adding any special type of irrigation or lighting system, or will you install a water feature?

## FINDING HELP AND INFORMATION

**6** **Resource and Aid Questions:** Where can you turn for expert advice? Do you have current books, periodicals, and catalogs containing information you'll require about the plants and garden techniques? Does your garden retailer have knowledgeable staff able to assist your decisions and answer your questions? Have you contacted your local USDA or Agriculture Canada extension office? Are there gardening classes available locally? Are there local experts on radio or television, in newspapers, or available electronically to whom you can turn with your questions?

Afiter mulling over your natural gardening possibilities, it's time to create your garden plan. This chapter takes you through the entire process, from garden concept to design reality. At the end, you'll have a representative drawing of a garden that fits your purpose, suits the scale of your home and site, matches your natural garden theme, and can be installed all at once or phased in over time, depending on your resources and skills.

**Creating a garden plan relies on your observation and a creative spirit, more than artistic skills**

Working on paper—or using a landscape design computer software program—allows you to experiment with the size and placement of various garden features, boundaries, and planting combinations before your hands ever touch the soil. You can integrate your natural garden into a larger design or plan your entire landscape as a natural garden. Your garden plan is a blueprint for building your garden. It is a handy reference when you plan the size of features and choose the type, amount, color, and texture of building materials. Your plan also guides the planting phase of your new garden. Use it to arrange trees, shrubs, ground covers, perennials, and annuals at appropriate spacing and in artful combinations.

# From Concept to Reality

You'll be able to use your garden plan to create shopping lists of building materials and plants you'll need before beginning your installation. If you choose to seek assistance for some or all of the project, your garden plan allows you to present your specific ideas to a contractor or landscaper. In some locales, a garden plan is required to obtain building permits.

One of the goals of the natural garden is that it blends effortlessly into its environment. To achieve this for your garden, you must gain an understanding of the subtleties of design that soften the edges between various landscape areas, between your house and your garden, and between your landscape and its surroundings. The principles presented in this chapter will help you understand how to establish boundaries and levels, use color and form, mix textures, and choose materials and plants that will increase both function and beauty in your garden.

*A sea of red, pink, and white valerian bloom across the floor of this natural garden inspired by a western meadow.*

## USE AND THEME

Y ou have set some goals concerning how you want to use your garden and how you want your garden to look. Now you are ready to decide how to accomplish these goals. Your site, desires, and resources all play a part in your decisions.

*(Right) What better setting for a child's imagination than their own whimsical playhouse set in a natural, woodland landscape? Let them plant some of their favorite flowers and start to grow fond memories.*

*(Bottom) Your vision of a natural garden should include areas to enjoy, mingle, and entertain. Use paths and patios to entice visitors to explore nature.*

Every site offers different issues. You may want to integrate your natural garden into your present landscape, you may face the blank slate found in a new development, you may want to enhance an existing natural area, or you may have an older home with an established landscape requiring a completely fresh look. With careful consideration, you'll discover what is best for your site.

If you are landscaping an established home, installing a natural garden may require you to remove existing elements such as overgrown plantings, paths, decks, and overtaxed

irrigation systems. Because it's often best to save an established tree or usable patio, you may want to consider ways to incorporate existing features into your new style and theme. Think of ways to design around existing features. Lawns can be removed, made smaller, or incorporated into a meadow; paths and masonry can be resurfaced; trees can be made the centerpiece of a shade garden.

Climate is an all-important factor in the design of any land-scape. Spend some more time in your yard tracking the sun and wind at several different times of day and different seasons of the year. Establish ideal locations for various functions. For example, locate the protected areas free of wind where you might want to place your lounging area or place delicate plants that need shelter.

Finalize your decision on your garden theme. It will help establish the overall ambiance and influences your choice of plants, structural features, finish materials, and garden accessories. Choice of theme is influenced by your geographic region, specific location, style of home, and favorite plants.

$S$cale—the size of objects and space in relation to one another and to the landscape as a whole—influences both the dimension of your garden and its appearance relative to your site and home. **SCALE AND SCOPE**

Keep your project in scale with your home as you experiment with different garden elements. Plants and structural features should both meet your needs and remain proportional to the size of the house and surrounding landscape. Always consider the mature height of your plants.

A garden filled with low, petite plantings would appear out of place in front of a multi-storied modern home. Similarly, a small house might look lost behind large shrubs and towering trees. A large garden generally needs tall plants to create balance. Smaller plants usually scale nicely with a tiny garden. The scale of planting beds should be appropriate to nearby paths, walls, and structures. Match wide beds with a generous deck, and a narrow border with a small patio.

There's an easy and inexpensive way to visualize the correct scale for all your garden elements. Take photographs of your site and make enlarged photocopies of your pictures. On the photocopies, draw new planting areas and structural features to scale. Rough in individual plants, using their mature height and general form. Experiment with various sizes until a good balance is found among the different elements.

Scope is the size of your project in terms of your skills, schedule, and resources. It includes all aspects: planning, site preparation, lighting and irrigation installation, plant and material selection, building, planting, and ongoing care. Remember, large garden projects can be done in phases. Your garden plan will help you keep your phased project on track as time passes.

*Consider the size of all garden accessories in terms of their scale within your garden. An Asian theme is equally appropriate for the stylized bonsai representation of nature found indoors in a container and as a theme garden for a large landscape. Only their scale is different.*

## BOUNDARIES AND TERRACES

*(Right) Create boundaries where none exist. Incorporate changes in level and elevation to help complete the illusion. Here, a fieldstone wall has just been completed. Soon, it will be back-filled with rich soil to create a raised bed ready for planting.*

Every garden has boundaries to define its edges. Boundaries divide and define space, create privacy, delineate use, and help create rhythm. They include paths, fences, walls, terraces, the outline of planting areas, and such structures as patios and decks.

There are few straight lines in nature; curve paths, make fence tops and walls uneven, round patios, and soften edges with plantings.

Go out on your site and create physical representations. Use a garden hose, stakes and string, or a line of flour to mark out future boundaries. Use cardboard boxes to mimic walls or hedges. Look at your proposed boundary from all sides before making your final decision.

*A rule, stakes, note-book, and sketch pad are important tools to have at hand when planning new garden bound-aries.*

Besides separating spaces, paths also provide access to and through your garden. When determining their width and materials, keep in mind that you'll need comfortable access to every garden space and to your home in all kinds of weather.

Fencing and wall styles vary by region and community. Choose materials to match your garden theme and set the tone for your garden. Walls and fences are perfect backdrops for specimen plants or supports for vines. Once grown in, an informal hedge is a wonderful living fence.

*A Pacific northwestern garden glorious with fiery azalea and feathery ferns contrasts with the massive stone wall that hides a utility area beyond.*

Hillside sites present a unique opportunity to "turn lemons into lemonade." Install terraces, retaining walls, and a set of steps to transform steep grades into striking and welcoming gardens. Terraces form level tiers of usable space while retaining soil and slowing runoff; steps are practical and inviting. Both add strong visual elements. Always check local codes before installing retaining walls. Use regionally appropriate materials to create natural-looking terraces. Local fieldstone is a superb choice for walls and terraces as it blends with its surroundings effortlessly and has timeless appeal. Wood, though more prone to decay than stone, is practical for some retaining walls and blends well with cottage, wood-land, and coastal garden themes. Another option is to build a wall of concrete blocks and cover it with facing stones for a natural look. Soften the edges of your terraces with cascades of low-growing, horizontal, and trailing plants.

## CHOOSING PAVING AND TERRACE MATERIALS

Paths, patios, terraces, and walls offer you a wonderful opportunity to add local materials to your garden. Think about the color, texture, durability, and availability of all materials. Strive for harmony with the region, your home, and your garden theme, and follow these easy steps:

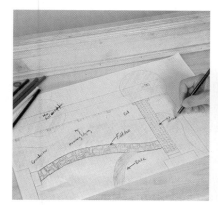

**1** Choose paving materials that are appropriate to the garden theme, will wear well, and are appropriate to the intended use. Match surface materials with natural textures.

**2** Visit supply outlets and garden centers to determine the availability of raw materials for construction of terrace walls.

**3** Choose between paving with concrete, brick, or rounded stone. For minor paths, choose gravel, bark chips, or other loose materials.

**4** Take samples to evaluate colors in your garden. Think about their suitability under various weather conditions.

**5** Consider options for terracing with aggregate block, timbers, or planks and posts. Note installation requirements, care needs, and life spans.

**6** Opt whenever possible for the natural look: dry-stacked fieldstone for walls, divisions, raised beds, and terraces.

## COLOR AND FORM

*(Below) The blazing fire of a mounded azalea dominates this meadow of blue-eyed grass along a woodland boundary. The azalea's springtime color soon will fade, and highlights will dot the field with the grass's tiny blue, yellow, and white flowers.*

Color stirs up a strong, personal, emotional response. What colors would you like to see in your garden? Consider the color of foliage and flowers along with the colors of your home and paving, finishing materials, and other structural features.

Imitate nature's subtle shadings and her bold statements. Note seasonal rhythms and how your garden's color will change with the seasons. Blooming flowers and the cycle of deciduous leaves supply a changing color show through the year. Include plenty of nature's favorite color—green. Foliage unifies the garden and provides a backdrop for seasonal color. Evergreen plants add color in the winter months. In arid regions, gray green and silver gray foliage becomes noteworthy.

Use color to create visual movement in your garden. Strong, vibrant colors draw the eye, while pastels tend to blend into the background. Light affects color as well. Strong, sunlit areas require bold colors, while shady nooks are well served by pastels.

Form is the plant's shape and growth habit. Distinctive forms are described as upright, mounded, spreading, arching, and bushy. Form makes plants useful for specific functions. Low-spreading plants make great ground covers; dense, upright plants make superior screens.

Use plant form to create harmony, contrast, and lend authenticity to your garden theme. Repetition of form provides unity and gives certain natural landscapes their unique quality. Some plants evoke geographic regions. The prairie is a sea of upright grasses and wildflowers, the woodland a forest of straight tree trunks. Add the occasional accent plant in a contrasting form to keep your garden visually interesting.

*(Above) Choosing plants with a distinctive shape helps a natural garden mirror its environment. The distinctive round form of day lily is a natural complement to the round, desert boulders.*

*(Bottom) Massed plantings, here California poppy, enliven the landscape with color. Consider naturalized bulbs, Icelandic poppy, and other bright-colored species for meadow and prairie themes.*

## CHOOSING PLANTS WITH A COLOR WHEEL

Color enlivens your garden. Use a color wheel, available at art-supply stores, to discover eye-catching color combinations. Colors that appear next to each other on the wheel are analogous—they blend together harmoniously and create a restful feeling. Colors across the wheel are complementary—they create contrast and add excitement to a design. Consider the colors of flowers, foliage, structures, walls, terraces, and paving materials when choosing color combinations, and follow these basic steps:

**1** Use a color wheel as you choose plants. Your first selection should be from the primary colors, followed by an analogous hue, then by its complement. Here, million bells 'Cherry Pink' is the primary color, with bush lantana 'Yellow Gold' as an analogous color, and vervain 'Homestead Purple' and Swan river daisy 'Harmony' chosen for their complementary colors.

**2** At the site, place plants into the bed in their containers. The planting shown is casual, and plants are grouped to make sinuous color zones.

**3** As the bed grows, empty spaces between plants will fill, and the borders between the plants will merge. In time, the vervain will spill down the drystack stone wall creating a flood of contrasting color.

## TEXTURE AND DEFINITION

Texture—the visual quality of leaves and surfaces—can be fine, medium, or coarse. Common words to describe textures are soft, prickly, smooth, rough, and bold. While color and form have a dramatic influence in your garden, texture also can make a big difference. Aim for an attractive interplay of fine, medium, and coarse textures. Contrast plants with hard-textured structural features and paving materials.

Plants with fine texture often have masses of tiny leaves or fernlike, branching foliage. Fine-textured plants also make striking accents. Think of a glade of ferns in a woodland garden or meadow grasses among bright wildflowers.

Plants with coarse texture are eye-catching, strong, and dramatic. Use them to create focal points in your garden.

A plant's texture helps define its role in the garden. Fine-textured plants soften the hard lines and surfaces of structural features. Install these plants at boundary and building edges to help blend structures into a natural garden. Massings of fine- or medium-textured plants lead your eye through the design. Arrange a group of the same plant along a path or at the back of the garden to encourage people to move through the space. Coarse-textured accent plants arrest your eye and cause you to pause. Place a coarse-textured plant near a bench to provide a place for both the eye and body to rest.

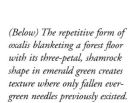

*(Top) Cacti often are thought of as stark, simple forms—after desert storms pass, their colorful blooms burst open, matching the profuse wildflowers of desert annual and perennial plants.*

*(Below) The repetitive form of oxalis blanketing a forest floor with its three-petal, shamrock shape in emerald green creates texture where only fallen evergreen needles previously existed.*

*Creating texture in a natural garden balances color, foliage, and form. Here, a coastal garden erupts with blooming ice plant and perennial herbs, a textural counterpoint to nearby salt-bleached driftwood.*

## CREATING YOUR GARDEN PLAN

N ow you are ready to document your ideas on a garden plan. You can draw a plan on paper or use computer software developed for landscape design. To draw a plan on paper, gather together scaled graph paper, colored pencils, your garden measurements, and a list of desired plants [see Creating a Planting Planner, pg. 33]. If you experimented with photographs of your site for scale or boundary placements in your garden, gather that information as well, and follow these steps:

**1** On scaled graph paper, draw the outline of the garden. Indicate features and plants to be retained. Make photocopies of this base plan.

**2** Lay tracing paper over a photocopy, then experiment with the location of the elements until you are satisfied that they fit your purpose and intended use. Evaluate for scale, views, and access.

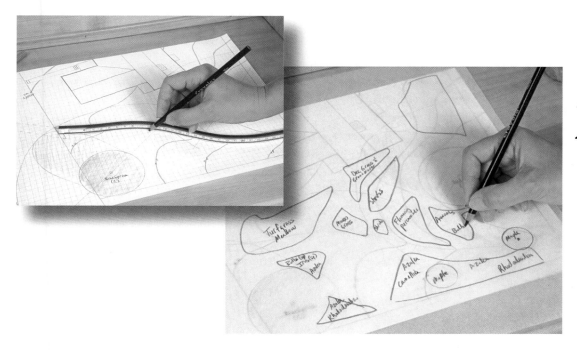

**3** On a clean overlay, position new boundaries, grade changes, and planting areas. Indicate new structural features and significant accessories.

**4** Use a different colored pencil for each type of plant, and space them according to the needs of each plant. Draw a circle to indicate its mature size and spread.

## OVER, UNDER, AND AROUND

Choose specific plants as a final step before taking your plan to the garden. Remember the principle of "the right plant for the right place." Select plants that are well-adapted to your plant hardiness zone, climate, microclimate, and growing conditions. Include alternates when you create your plant list, so you may substitute an item.

When planting combinations, always consider color, form, and texture. Remember how each plant will help define your natural garden theme. To avoid future pruning and preserve each plant's natural shape, choose shrubs and trees with mature sizes in scale with your site.

Track each plant's visual impact throughout the year. For flowering plants, keep in mind bloom times as well as colors. Remember that some plants go dormant and disappear from the garden for a time each year. Compare evergreens, which provide their consistent look and texture all year round, to deciduous plants with their showy, seasonal foliage changes.

In nature, plants grow in layers. Imitate nature to create a garden that appears both casual and spontaneous.

Trees form the garden's ceiling, or overstory. They provide beauty, shade, and structure, and they blend the garden into the surrounding landscape. Smaller trees, shrubs, large perennials, ferns, vines, and large grasses form your garden's understory. Use them to screen, enclose space, soften structures, and add seasonal appeal. Ground covers, small grasses, some ferns, smaller perennials, and annuals form your garden's floor.

For the best appearance, group plants in odd numbers. Plant in curves, masses, and natural drifts avoiding straight lines and symmetrical groupings.

*Paving makes a statement in a natural garden. The massive pavers used here convey their permanence and strength, while baby's-tears softens the edges.*

*A mowed meadow of mixed perennial wild grasses functions as turfgrass in a natural garden. Mow the entire area or mow a path to direct travel through taller grass left to grow and form seed heads.*

# CREATING A PLANTING PLANNER

| Category _____ | | | Page ___ |
|---|---|---|---|
| **Plant Description** | **Needs** | **Care** | **Notes** |
| Name:<br>Form:<br>Mature Size:<br>Foliage Color/Texture:<br>Bloom Color:<br>Bloom Season:<br>Dormant Season: | Sun:<br>Soil Type/pH:<br>Spacing:<br>When to Plant:<br>Special Needs: | Spring:<br>Summer:<br>Autumn:<br>Winter: | |
| Name:<br>Form:<br>Mature Size:<br>Foliage Color/Texture:<br>Bloom Color:<br>Bloom Season:<br>Dormant Season: | Sun:<br>Soil Type/pH:<br>Spacing:<br>When to Plant:<br>Special Needs: | Spring:<br>Summer:<br>Autumn:<br>Winter: | |
| Name:<br>Form:<br>Mature Size:<br>Foliage Color/Texture:<br>Bloom Color:<br>Bloom Season:<br>Dormant Season: | Sun:<br>Soil Type/pH:<br>Spacing:<br>When to Plant:<br>Special Needs: | Spring:<br>Summer:<br>Autumn:<br>Winter: | |
| Name:<br>Form:<br>Mature Size:<br>Foliage Color/Texture:<br>Bloom Color:<br>Bloom Season:<br>Dormant Season: | Sun:<br>Soil Type/pH:<br>Spacing:<br>When to Plant:<br>Special Needs: | Spring:<br>Summer:<br>Autumn:<br>Winter: | |
| Name:<br>Form:<br>Mature Size:<br>Foliage Color/Texture:<br>Bloom Color:<br>Bloom Season:<br>Dormant Season: | Sun:<br>Soil Type/pH:<br>Spacing:<br>When to Plant:<br>Special Needs: | Spring:<br>Summer:<br>Autumn:<br>Winter: | |
| Name:<br>Form:<br>Mature Size:<br>Foliage Color/Texture:<br>Bloom Color:<br>Bloom Season:<br>Dormant Season: | Sun:<br>Soil Type/pH:<br>Spacing:<br>When to Plant:<br>Special Needs: | Spring:<br>Summer:<br>Autumn:<br>Winter: | |
| Name:<br>Form:<br>Mature Size:<br>Foliage Color/Texture:<br>Bloom Color:<br>Bloom Season:<br>Dormant Season: | Sun:<br>Soil Type/pH:<br>Spacing:<br>When to Plant:<br>Special Needs: | Spring:<br>Summer:<br>Autumn:<br>Winter: | |

A planting planner is a useful tool both when you look for plants and as a future reference for using your garden. The planner succinctly details information about each plant you will install in your garden. It becomes your plant shopping list. It also is a reminder of seasonal plant needs and care requirements and will help you avoid digging up dormant plants or pulling out their new sprouts. It also serves as your reminder of major care tasks by season. If you plan to install your garden in phases, it records the plants needed and allows you to keep an eye out for unusual or rare items to add to your landscape.

I

t's now time to get on the land and create your new garden. As you add paths, install utilities, and outline planting areas, you'll see your plan begin to come to life. These permanent elements provide the "bones" of the garden, to which you'll add the plants.

Before you begin, check your garden plan to prioritize your installation tasks. Devise a schedule to keep yourself organized and eliminate extra shopping trips. Coordinating tasks that use similar skills and materials is an efficient way to make the most of your time and resources. Generally, choose between preparing the entire yard and then adding the plants, or preparing and planting sections of the yard in phases.

On the pages that follow are step-by-step instructions for each task you need to perform to make your site attractive, useful, and ready for planting. The complexity of your design will determine the number of tasks involved in preparing your site. All should be completed prior to installing plants in your garden. These preparation tasks include grading and creating terraces, building paths, and installing drainage, irrigation, and lighting systems. Landscape professionals refer to a garden's features, and to the systems that allow it to function, as its hardscape. They call its plants the greengoods.

Also in this chapter are ideas for the plants and accessories that will help you enhance your yard for birds and butterflies. As you prepare your garden, remember these wildlife friends. Avoid disrupting their current habitats during your garden preparation and consider various ways to welcome these visitors to your yard. The addition of a few accessories makes all the difference to attracting local wildlife. There are a number of elements from which to choose, including bird feeders, water features, shelters, or the right mixture of plants.

Tempting as it is to start planting, you'll find your garden does better over the years if you prepare the soil and add any amendments before installing your plants. The chapter ends with simple steps for preparing your soil for the plants to come.

**Before you can begin planting, you'll need to establish a framework of terraces, paths, utilities, and planting areas**

# Preparing the Site

*Preparing a site for planting may include amending its soil, terracing and building walls, adding watering and lighting systems, and installing paths and beds. Here, a stairway of natural rock has been installed on a hillside site, improving access to the garden.*

## GRADES AND ELEVATIONS

Steps, retaining walls, and terraces transform slopes into unique and attractive garden possibilities. Establishing levels or a few steps on a gentle slope provide access, add visual interest, and may help reduce excess runoff that causes erosion.

Check and comply with local code and permit requirements if you plan to install any wall higher than 18 inches (45 cm). If you're contemplating a retaining wall higher than 3 feet (90 cm) or dealing with a very steep incline, unstable soil, drainage, or uneven terrain, consult an engineer before proceeding.

The surface of a step is called the tread; the vertical part is its riser. When designing steps, keep the tread proportional to the riser. Generally, pair shorter risers with deeper treads. For example, a 14-inch (35-cm) tread with a 6-inch (15-cm) riser is a comfortable stride. Other fitting combinations are 11-inch (28-cm) treads and 7-inch (18-cm) risers, and 18-inch (45-cm) treads with 4-inch (10-cm) risers.

If you have a gentle slope, installing a low terrace or short retaining wall can be a great do-it-yourself project. Start by choosing the best kind of retaining wall material for your garden theme. Then determine location. Decide whether to retain a bank of soil with a single wall or a series of terraces. Generally, the steeper the slope, the more terraces you need.

*Take advantage of any natural elevation variations when you plan your garden. Here, a rock wall of an old quarry has been planted with trailing plants and clusters of tall bulbs, softening the face and framing the bulb and annual planting below.*

Measure changes in elevation on your site by driving a short stake at the highest point of the slope and a tall stake at its lowest point. Attach string flush with the ground to the short stake, pull it down the slope, and attach it to the tall stake. Use a line level on the string to make its attachment point even with that of the short stake. The vertical length of the tall stake, from its intersection with the ground to the point where the string is tied, is the rise—change in elevation over the slope. The horizontal length of the string, from short to tall stake, is the run. A series of such measurements may be necessary on long or steep sites.

To fit your terraces to the slope, decide the height of each terrace. Then divide that height into the total rise to find the number of terraces you'll need to install. Alternatively, divide the number of terraces you want into the rise to determine the height of each terrace. Either way, the distance between terraces is found by dividing their number into the run. You can make adjustments as you construct the project.

## INSTALLING TERRACES AND LEVELS

**B**efore obtaining materials, determine the number, height, and width of your terraces. Consult with your local home improvement store or garden center to determine the amount of stone, sand, and aggregate you'll need. Clear the site of turf grass and other vegetation. These guidelines illustrate the construction of a dry-stacked stone island terrace built from fieldstone on a flat site. A similar approach would be used for hillside terraces. Gather together a line level, shovel, stakes, string, and tamping tool, and follow these basic steps:

**1** Mark the terrace's location with stakes. Fasten a string between stakes to mark its final height. Verify the string is level. Excavate a trench 8–12 in. (20–30 cm) deep along the run of the terrace, using a trenching shovel. Reserve the excavated soil as fill for the finished terrace.

**2** Compact the base soil of the trench using a tamping tool until it is firm. Add a 4–6-in. (10–15-cm) layer of sand to the base of the trench. Sand will permit you to precisely level the first course of stones of the terrace.

**3** Set and level the first course of stones, using a carpenter's liquid level for accuracy.

**4** Stack additional courses of fieldstone one-over-two, covering all joint spaces and stepping back each course 1–2 in. (25–50 mm) from the face. It's easier to set and precisely level two endstones, then fill the space between them to the level, than it is to work from one end to the other.

**5** Add aggregate behind the finished terrace wall to stabilize it and provide drainage. Fill the terrace with topsoil mixed with excavated soil from the trench. Add more topsoil before planting, as the terrace will settle and compact for several weeks after being filled.

## PATHS

Paths welcome visitors to your garden, invite exploration, and help set a tone for your garden theme. As a design element, they create lines for your eye to follow and form boundaries. On the practical side, they provide access through your garden and to your home or decks and patios, and they are suitable both for leisurely strolls and trips with a wheelbarrow hauling tools and plants.

Consider the path's use before you decide on its size and appearance. Plan a circulation pattern that works for your yard and your physical needs. Some paths will be a delightful journey through the garden, used primarily in daylight during fair weather. Other paths provide access to the house, toolshed, or garage and must be negotiated day or night in all kinds of weather. Access paths that must be used year-round and which are sited close to your home should be made of durable material that is weather-tolerant and relates visually to the structure.

As you get farther into your site, garden paths should invite a slow trek to enjoy nature. These paths can be more circuitous and constructed of less durable materials than access paths. Plan a payoff for the end of every path: an accent plant, a water feature, or a seating area to rest, reflect, and enjoy the garden's beauty.

*Flagstone paths are easily installed on a bed of sand 4-inches (10 cm) thick. Use a straight edge to set stones even and level. Plant a low-growing ground cover into the space between stones to complete the path's look. Here, isotoma was used; other good pathway choices include dwarf club moss, mock strawberry, and wooly thyme.*

The heavier its use, the wider and safer you'll want to make your path. A path 5 feet (1.5 m) wide—picture a city sidewalk—allows two people to walk side by side comfortably. In most cases, something narrower is usually sufficient—plan paths to be 30–48 inches (75–120 cm) wide.

Myriad materials can be used for paths in a natural garden. Choose materials appropriate for your use and your garden's theme. Consider loose materials including bark chips, gravel, and crushed shells for seldom-used paths. For access paths, create a natural look that holds up to weather conditions, such as installed stone pieces with sand or ground cover plants filling breaks in the grout. A winding path of stepping-stones is charming in out-of-the-way parts of the garden and still provides safe access and secure footing.

## INSTALLING NATURAL PATHS

An informal curving path of flagstone adds a lovely and authentic visual element to a natural garden. Use the measurements on your garden plan to determine the quantity of stones and amounts you'll need of coarse sand and weed-barrier fabric. In this design, the installation of dwarf club moss between the stones adds to the natural look of the path. Gather together a shovel, tamping tool, measuring tape, level, rubber mallet, rake, and broom, and follow these steps:

**2** Lay 3 in. (75 mm) of coarse sand over the soil. Rake, level, and tamp.

**3** Set flagstones about 1–2 in. (25–50 mm) apart, bedding them into the sand until level. To size stones, score them with a chisel, then tap.

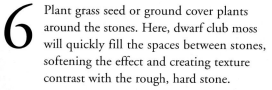

**1** Remove existing plants and excavate soil approximately 5 in. (13 cm) deep. Tamp the soil until it is compact and stable. Install weed-barrier fabric.

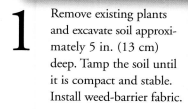

**4** Seat each stone by tapping it with a mallet. Check level and adjust as needed, adding or removing sand.

**5** Fill spaces between stones with a mix of sand and topsoil, using a rake and broom.

**6** Plant grass seed or ground cover plants around the stones. Here, dwarf club moss will quickly fill the spaces between stones, softening the effect and creating texture contrast with the rough, hard stone.

## DRAINAGE, IRRIGATION, AND LIGHTING

Increase the function and reduce the care required by your garden by installing drainage, irrigation, and lighting systems. Garden system supplies are available at most building supply and home improvement stores and at garden centers. Always check and comply with local building codes and permit requirements when planning and constructing your project. Identify and mark all underground utility lines before digging in their vicinity. Utilities provide a free service for locating underground pipes and electric lines.

Water often accumulates in low spots, at the base of slopes, or adjacent to paved surfaces. Correct excess drainage and standing water with easy-to-install PVC drain pipe. If your site drains too quickly, causing erosion or flooding, you may need to divert water away from structures before installing plants. Install a French drain—underground perforated drainage pipes in trenches dug along a structure's foundation and filled with gravel. They collect excess water and carry it away.

Because you've picked plants that thrive in your climate, your natural garden should survive with limited watering. In-ground irrigation systems save water and effort compared to hand watering. They eliminate excessive runoff and minimize the time spent managing hoses and sprinklers. Most operate with an automatic timer.

Low-voltage night lighting increases garden security, functionality, and beauty. Such lighting is economical and generally easy to install. Soft pools of light illuminating paths make the garden safer and more attractive. Landscape lights cast soft shadows and create interesting effects. Lights can extend your hours of garden use. You'll find yourself wanting to linger long after dusk.

*(Top) Impulse sprinklers are a choice for overhead watering of turf and ornamental grasses.*

*(Above) A dry streambed can become functional when rainfall is heavy. Use it as a decorative element in arid gardens, sloping the stream to direct water away from structures and your garden.*

*(Bottom) Low-voltage lighting illuminates a landscape as evening falls. It also aids safety where paths turn sharply or ascend steps.*

## CONTROLLING WATER FLOW AND INSTALLING DRAINAGE

Observe your garden after a hard rain to identify drainage patterns at your site. Consider installing drainage at spots where water stands on the surface for extended periods. Divert runoff whenever water flows quickly through your yard, erodes the topsoil, causes gullies to appear, or runs towards your home or other structures. Use your garden plan to determine the amount you'll need of pipe, gravel, and root-barrier or filter fabric. Gather together shovels and helpers to perform these simple-to-understand steps, some of which require strenuous effort:

### Installing French Drains

**1** Dig a U-shaped trench 18–24 in. (45–60 cm) deep at its center in the area to be drained, and 6–12 in. (15–30 cm) deep downslope.

**2** Cut perforated PVC drain pipe to fit. Lay the pipe on a gravel bed, hole side down. Run each end downslope to daylight or a dry well filled with stone. Glue sections with two-part PVC solvent and glue. Wrap the pipe with landscape fabric.

**3** Cover the drain with more gravel and another layer of landscape fabric to protect it from roots. Fill to the top of the trench with topsoil.

### Diverting Runoff

**1** Dig two parallel trenches 6 in. (15 cm) deep on either side of the gully, ending 6 in. (15 cm) above the bottom of the hill or slope.

**2** Line the space between the trenches with woven landscape filter fabric. Anchor the fabric edges in the trenches using large-diameter gravel.

**3** Cover the fabric on the gully with overlapping pavers, installed using a shingle-laid method. Cover the pavers and trenches with topsoil.

## INSTALLING IN-GROUND IRRIGATION

**1** From a water supply line, gate valve, and backflow prevention valve, trench and run 1-in. (25-mm) schedule 40 pipe to the control valve site. Trenching machines are available at equipment rental yards.

**A**n irrigation system can be a lifesaver when you're establishing new plantings or you experience a period of drought. To simplify your system design, group plants according to their water needs. In regions where freezing temperatures are likely, mount control valves below ground and include a drain valve at the lowest point in your system. Use your garden plan to measure your water coverage needs. Gather together shovels, a PVC pipe-cutting tool, and follow these steps:

**2** Install a ¾-in. (19-mm) threaded reducing bushing at the valve. Install separate control valves for each watering circuit. Use a ½-in. (13-mm) reducing bushing between each valve and the lines that run to the sprinkler heads or drip emitters.

**3** Cut the pipe to length. Seal any pipe joints using two-step PVC primer and solvent adhesive. Allow the joints to dry.

**4** Install a 90° street tee or ell fitting where you plan to position each irrigation head, using a threaded slip joint between the supply pipe and riser.

**5** Install sprinkler spray housings or drip system hose couplers atop each riser, using three wraps of Teflon® tape around each threaded fitting.

**6** Turn on the gate valve and the sprinkler manifold to clear the line of debris. Turn off and install the sprinkler heads or the drip emitters. Mount and set the controller.

## INSTALLING LOW-VOLTAGE LIGHTING

**N**ight lighting lends a soft glow and lets you enjoy evenings in your garden. Draw a simple map to attain your desired effect and keep it for future reference. For a natural look, use lights sparingly. Choose durable lights that will perform in any weather conditions. For safety, always attach 12-volt D.C. transformers to all-weather ground fault circuit interrupter (GFCI) protected outlets. Splice cable with waterproof splice kits. Check and comply with all code and permit requirements and follow these steps:

**1** Identify or install an 120-volt A.C. outlet at the transformer location. Low-voltage lighting requires all 12-volt D.C. transformers be connected to a GFCI outlet. Test the circuit.

**2** Dig a trench 6–8 in. (15–20 cm) deep from the outlet along the path of the lighting system. Lighting trenches should be separate from irrigation trenches.

**3** Lay 12–2 direct burial 12-volt cable in the trench to the center of the circuit. Wiring runs should be less than 100 ft. (30 m) long in total. Splice cable to each end, creating a T.

**4** Splice fixtures to the supply cable at each location with direct-burial connectors. Reserve 3 ft. (90 cm) of slack cable around each fixture's base.

**5** Use the slack in the cable to position the light fixtures, then install them in the soil. Cover the run with mulch, as desired.

**6** Install plants around lighting fixtures to integrate them into the garden. Adjust the fixture positions as the plants grow.

## WELCOMING BIRDS AND BUTTERFLIES

An opportunity to enjoy birds and butterflies is one purpose of many natural gardens. Butterflies provide a beneficial service to your garden by pollinating flowers. In turn, even a small backyard butterfly garden provides them with a sanctuary and promotes the survival of local butterfly populations, a benefit to the entire environment. Birds add excitement to the garden with their cheerful songs and quick movements. Welcome birds to your garden by providing four essential elements—food, shelter, nesting sites, and water.

Bird feeders are a wonderful attraction for birds. Choose a style that suits your garden theme and regularly fill it with seed. Also choose plants that provide a feast for birds: plant trees, shrubs, vines, grasses, and perennials that produce edible berries, seeds, nuts, and nectar. Native plants are your best choice for attracting local birds, although many birds also will consume more exotic fare. It's a thrill to see a flock of goldfinches arrive to feast on your coreopsis after it has gone to seed or a hummingbird stop by to sip nectar from your columbine. Many birds also eat insects. Acrobatic swallows catching pesky flying insects is a welcome sight on a summer evening.

Birds need cover to feel at home. Create welcoming habitats by planting an overstory of trees and an understory of shrubs, vines, and grasses that provide shelter from wind, weather, and predators. Evergreens provide protection in the winter.

Once you've come to know your local birds, you'll want them to move right in and raise their young. Install rustic birdhouses and nest boxes. Verify specific birdhouse height and nesting style requirements for bird species that frequent your garden; they vary greatly among birds. Locate birdhouses out of reach of pets and other predators. Trees, including dogwood and American holly, provide food as well as nesting space; you supply the plant and the birds will do the rest.

The arrival of butterflies is a magical part of summer. From where do butterflies come? Caterpillars! Plant food sources, including hollyhock, goldenrod, and windflower, and you may have the delight of watching a butterfly emerge from its chrysalis. To attract multitudes of butterflies, plant nectar-rich flowers in sunny exposures. Certain flowers, including asters, coneflowers, Oregon grape, and viburnum, are butterfly magnets. Provide a shallow water source with protection from high winds. Butterflies appreciate flat surfaces near water where they can bask in the sun.

*Butterflies and moths often rival flowers in their beauty. A little time spent researching local species will reveal their preferred choices for food. Plant the species that attract them and your natural garden will be a magnet to butterflies.*

## WATER FEATURES

Water is an essential element of wildlife habitats. Birds need water for drinking and bathing. A water feature—fountain, birdbath, shallow saucer, or pond—is a beautiful addition to a natural garden and a great location for bird watching. Place water features where they can be viewed comfortably from your house or a seating area within the yard. Birdbaths should be 3 feet (90 cm) from the ground and in the open to avoid predators. Basins with diameters of 2–3 feet (60–90 cm) will attract a community of bathers. Plan an irregularly shaped pond and work local stone into the edging, in keeping with your garden theme. Create gentle inclines or a pebble beach to allow birds to wade, and surround your pond with sheltering plants.

## CREATING BIRD HABITATS

**I**t's easy to create a habitat for birds while you're designing a garden that appeals to people. Native and regionally adapted plants will appeal to your local feathered friends. Plan a diverse group of plants with about 50 percent evergreens for summer nesting and winter cover to attract birds to your garden, and take these measures:

**A** Plant overstory and understory plants—trees, shrubs, vines, perennials, grasses—to provide a complete bird habitat.

**B** Provide year-round food sources with plants that yield nectar, fruit, and seeds. Add feeders to supplement their diet. Maintain various feeding stations for different kinds of birds.

**C** Install appropriate nesting sites and birdhouses out of reach of pets and predators. Check nesting preferences of local birds.

**D** Add a birdbath or other water feature. Keep birdbaths at least 3 ft. (90 cm) above the ground and away from any vegetative cover that provides camouflage for predators.

## ESTABLISHING PLANTING AREAS

To create your planting beds, transfer the measurements from your garden plan. Use wooden stakes and string, a garden hose, or even flour to outline their location and shape. Install underground systems—drainage, irrigation, and lighting—prior to preparing your planting areas [see Drainage, Irrigation, and Lighting, pg. 40].

If you are remodeling an existing landscape, remove existing plants, lawn turf, and weeds with a sharp spade and a sod lifter. Alternatively, smother and remove grass or weeds with a layer of soil, mulch, or clear plastic. As a quicker option to destroying grass and weeds, consider using a short-duration biodegradable herbicide after weighing personal safety and environmental considerations.

If you have a new home, construction may have severely compacted the soil. In such cases, loosen the soil throughout the entire planting area. Always remove any debris or rocks found below the surface of the soil. Ideally, prior to planting you want loose, unobstructed soil about 1-foot (30-cm) deep.

Most natural gardens are designed with plants that will thrive in the native soil. Your need to amend your soil with organic matter will depend on the soil type at your site and the plants you've chosen [see Understand the Soil, pg. 15]. Organic matter—shredded leaves, leaf mold, aged manure, and organic compost—decomposes into rich humus that provides nutrients to the plants and facilitates the transfer of both air and moisture. If your soil requires amending with organic matter, perform this task before planting. Peat moss has been used for centuries as a soil amendment; however, it's best to find alternatives for this non-renewable resource.

Compost—decomposed organic matter—is a popular soil amendment for natural gardens. In clay soils, compost helps break up dense particles, improving structure and drainage. In sandy soils, it helps increase moisture retention. Because compost often is rich in nitrogen, phosphorus, and potassium plus other trace elements, vital micronutrients, and beneficial microorganisms, it plays a big role in boosting soil fertility.

You can purchase compost or make your own by setting up a system to recycle garden and vegetable waste. Check at your local nursery or garden center for the best amendments for your soil and the plants you've decided to grow.

*Most gardens contain beds and borders. This colorful spring border captures the spirit of nature in a small-space garden located within an urban area.*

**AMENDING THE SOIL**

$S$oil amendments add nutrients, improve texture, modify the acid-alkaline balance, and change the ratio of mineral elements and organic components. Amend soil that has been compacted, stripped of topsoil, or lacks organic matter. Water the planting area the evening before you add soil amendments. The soil should be slightly moist, neither soggy nor powder dry. Gather together a shovel, spading fork, and rake. Wear gloves and sun protection, and follow these steps:

**1** Clear the planting area of weeds, turf, and other plants. Loosen soil and remove obstructions at least 1 ft. (30 cm) deep.

**2** Use a soil test kit according to its package instructions to test your unamended soil. Take your soil sample from the side of a hole, 8–10 in. (20–25 cm) below the surface. Follow the kits recommendation for the amount and type of amendment to be added.

**3** Spread organic matter and other amendments across the planting area in a layer 2–4 in. (50–100 mm) deep. Use a spading fork or rotary tiller to work the organic matter into the loosened soil.

**4** Rake the bed until the soil surface is level and smooth. It is ready to plant.

Now is the time to head to the nursery or garden center and load up on plants. This chapter offers guidelines and step-by-step instructions for choosing healthy plants that suit your garden theme and planting them after you take them home. Plants are available in different forms—from seeds, to bulbs, to various sizes of nursery container—and each is planted differently. Many annuals and wildflowers are best planted from seed. Bulbs should be planted several months before their blooming time, in autumn for spring-blooming bulbs and in spring for summer-blooming varieties. While seeds and bulbs take time to grow and bloom, they are wonderful additions to many natural gardens. Perennials, shrubs, vines, ferns, ground covers, and trees are sold in various sizes of nursery container. Specialty plants for wetland sites and arid gardens have unique installation needs as well. A specific planting method is presented here for each plant form.

> Give your garden a great start by choosing healthy plants and using proper planting techniques

# Planting Natural Settings

Return to your garden plan and review your planting planner to guide your selection. Check nurseries, garden centers, direct merchants, and specialty plant sources to find the plants you need. A search may be necessary to locate certain species. Even if your heart is set on a particular plant, be flexible and modify your plan based on what's available. If your local retailer has a wonderful, vigorous plant with similar traits and requirements, you could make a substitution. Take advantage of the wide range of available plants at your nursery and garden center to create attractive combinations. Remember to pursue local native plants— they're tailor made for your region—while considering well-adapted imports as well.

Consider the time it takes to perform the planting tasks as you choose your plants. It's best to select only the number of plants that you'll be able to install in the following few days. If you find yourself with plants waiting to go into the ground for an extended period, set up a holding area. Keep the plants shaded and watered as they await planting.

*Purple coneflower is a staple of many natural gardens. It's prized for its large size, colorful blooms, and seed heads that attract birds.*

## NATIVE-INSPIRED PLANTS

One approach to natural gardening is to plant exclusively native species. Natives are those plants that once—and perhaps still—grow wild in your area. The popularity of regional gardening has brought gardening with native plants into the limelight. Natives are ideally suited to your region, they'll blend well with the surrounding landscape, and they appeal to local wildlife.

A natural style approach uses both native plants and those from other regions [see Beautiful Natural Gardens, pg. 1]. Many cultivated plants are native to other locations or were created by grower breeding. They are good choices if they are adapted to your hardiness zone, climate, soil type, and site conditions, and suit your garden theme. This approach, for example, pairs an Asian woodland resident with a North American woodland wildflower, or a Florida native with a tropical plant from South Africa. The results can be stunning.

Avoid introducing invasive plants into natural areas. If your garden is adjacent to a natural habitat, choose plants carefully. Certain species are banned in some locales due to their threat of hazard to native plant populations.

Check restrictions from direct merchants when ordering or when moving with a favorite plant. Some plant bans are required to prevent the spread of unwelcome pests and diseases, rather than any issue with the plant itself.

When choosing plants, you may have noticed that many plants are given cultivar—cultivated variety—names that appear in single quotes, for example, 'Moonbeam' yarrow or 'Bright Star' purple coneflower. Such plants have been selected because of their desirable traits. When a plant has "improved" characteristics, such as longer flowering times or bigger blooms, it is given a special name. Each plant sold under such a name is nearly or exactly identical genetically.

In your quest for inspiration, visit natural areas for ideas, always leaving wild plants where you find them. Seek out nurseries that offer a good selection of nursery-propagated plants similar to the ones you've seen growing in the wild. It is a sad fact that some plants, especially rare wildflowers, desert cacti, and bulbs, now are threatened by extinction due to overzealous collection by plant poachers.

*This white-flowered blue-flag iris is a popular plant for shoreline plantings around water features or in marshy settings in the landscape. It is a native of marshes in the central United States.*

## SELECTING HEALTHY PLANTS

Examine plants at the nursery or garden center before deciding to bring them home, just as you would thump a melon at the grocery. A young, vigorous plant has a head start in your garden and can make an easier transition into your landscape. Ask the staff if the plant is available in a size you're seeking. Carefully check plant labels against your planting planner for correct names—many species appear similar without their blooms. Verify heights, bloom colors, and the quantity you require, referring to your planting planner, and follow these steps:

**1** Look for plants that are compact, uniformly shaped, vigorous, and sturdy, avoiding any that are limp, lanky, or stunted.

**2** Examine the leaves for even, proper color and symmetrical spacing. Avoid those with broken or damaged stems.

**3** Reject plants with symptoms of pests or disease. Some signs to avoid are foliage or stems that contain holes, discoloration, or pests, or powdery looking, yellowed, or brown-spotted leaves.

**4** Gently slip the plant out of the container to look for firm, vigorous roots that still have room to grow. Plants with encircling roots or large roots growing out of the container drain holes have been held in stock too long.

## ANNUAL FLOWERS

Annuals complete their life cycle—sprouting, blooming, setting seed, and dying—in a single growing season. Their bright colors and profuse flowers make them ideal for use in your natural garden.

Choose annuals that fit your garden theme and are well suited to your plant hardiness zone, climate, soil, and site conditions [see Encyclopedia of Natural Garden Plants, pg. 79]. Cottage, meadow, prairie, and arid gardens often include a variety of colorful annuals as well as other plants and shrubs.

Annuals are available as seed, individual nursery containers, and in cell-packs grouped in flats. Nursery transplants produce nearly instant color in the garden. Many annuals, including poppies, however, have a taproot and should be grown from seed sown directly in the ground.

Growers breed annuals, called bedding plants, to produce masses of flowers on compact plants. Most bedding plants need loose, rich soil, fertilizing, and frequent watering to look their best. For natural gardens, choose annuals with simple flowers and an open graceful habit. Plant them in drifts, avoiding formal blocks of color.

Sow your annual meadows or prairies from seed, for reasons of economy and to save the time needed to plant large numbers of plants from nursery containers. For an expanse of one species, choose plants that aesthetically lend themselves to massing. For mixed plantings, pick plants that are similar in height and coordinate their bloom periods for consecutive displays of color.

In some regions hardy annuals self-sow —fling their seeds and return as volunteers.

*(Inset) Twine a birdhouse on a sturdy pole with morning glory and you'll serve wild birds two ways. The vine will discourage predators from reaching the nest, and the vine will produce edible seeds.*

*(Bottom) Blue marguerite is a herbaceous annual noted for its striking blue flowers and long blooming season. In mild-winter climates, it sometimes survives for several seasons.*

## PLANTING WILDFLOWERS FROM SEED

**1** Chill seeds in a sealed plastic container in the vegetable drawer of your refrigerator for 3–4 weeks before planting, if recommended on the package.

Growing wildflowers from seed is an economical method of creating a wildflower meadow or using wildflowers in other garden settings. Read seed packets, choosing only those recommended for your growing conditions. Some wildflower seeds require chilling, scarification, or soaking prior to planting. All seeds are perishable and sold with an expiration date. To grow any plant from seed, follow these steps:

**2** Prepare the planting area by removing competing weeds, rocks, and obstructions. Use a hoe or spade to loosen the soil to a depth of at least 6 in. (15 cm).

**3** Alternatively, use a garden tiller to work the soil and amendments prior to planting.

**4** Scatter seeds across the loose soil of the planting area using either your hand or a hand rotary spreader, depending on the area to be sown.

**6** Water using a hose nozzle set on mist. Repeat watering whenever the soil dries.

**5** Press the seed into firm soil contact to hasten germination, using the flat palms of your hands.

## ORNAMENTAL GRASSES, GROUND COVERS, AND FERNS

Texture is the hallmark of ornamental grasses, ground covers, and ferns. Most are grown for their year-round foliage. Used in mass—a drift of grass, a sweep of ground cover, a glade of ferns—they unify your design. Grasses and ferns also can be planted as accents. On the practical side, most of these plants are hardy specimens that thrive where other plants would struggle to survive.

Ornamental grasses, as opposed to turf grasses, are grown as perennial plants. They create varied levels to form screens, backgrounds, and accents. Their simple elegance adds movement and grace to many natural garden themes [see Encyclopedia of Natural Garden Plants, pg. 107].

Most ornamental grasses grow in full sun to partial shade. Adaptable and tough, grasses tolerate a wide range of soil types and growing conditions. Grasses are low maintenance; beyond an annual trim they require little attention. Their fibrous roots are adept at gleaning water from the soil, and they generally are drought-tolerant.

Ground covers spread to form a garden's floor. Ground cover plants come in a range of textures and heights, and can be deciduous or evergreen. Some produce vivid seasonal color. In addition to replacing high-maintenance turf, ground covers perform other desirable functions: they cool the soil, conserve moisture, reduce erosion, discourage weeds, and serve as a living mulch beneath trees and shrubs. From a design perspective, ground covers both unify and soften. A drift of plants can blend boundaries between planting areas and paths, merge structural features into the garden, and frame specimen trees. Ground covers are effective in most natural garden themes [see Encyclopedia of Natural Garden Plants, pg. 112].

Ferns, though delicate in appearance, happily grow in places where few other plants will thrive. Ferns are tough survivors; they've been around for hundreds of millions of years. A shady spot, poorly suited to sun-loving species, could be the perfect place for a verdant swath of ferns. Look for ferns at garden retailers that specialize in native and shade plants. Most ferns need moist, well-drained soil, high in organic matter. They are perfect companions to wildflowers and seasonal bulbs in a woodland garden [see Encyclopedia of Natural Garden Plants, pg. 115].

*(Inset) Ornamental grasses are long-lived perennials. They often feature distinctive seed heads, such as this one resembling the rattles of a rattlesnake.*

*(Bottom) A simple meadow of mixed native grasses and wildflowers creates a quiet respite.*

## PLANTING ORNAMENTAL GRASSES

Ornamental grasses are among the easiest plants to grow. Verify the spacing requirements of individual plants. Site them correctly—many grow quite large. Cut grasses annually to enjoy their graceful beauty year after year. Ornamental grasses are available in nursery containers or as bare-root divisions. Spring is the best time to plant most grasses; it provides a whole growing season for the plants to become established. To plant ornamental grasses from nursery containers, follow these easy steps:

**1** Prepare the planting area. Mark each planting point based on your garden plan. Dig holes as deep as the containers and slightly wider.

**2** Remove the plant from the nursery container. Set the plant in the hole so that its root crown is level with the surrounding soil surface and matches the soil level of the container. Add or remove soil as necessary to create proper depth.

**3** Fill the hole, using your hands to gently firm the soil around the crown. Water thoroughly at time of planting and keep the soil moist until the plant is established. Water thereafter whenever it becomes dry.

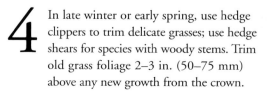

**4** In late winter or early spring, use hedge clippers to trim delicate grasses; use hedge shears for species with woody stems. Trim old grass foliage 2–3 in. (50–75 mm) above any new growth from the crown.

## PLANTING GROUND COVERS

**N**ew ground cover requires regular watering and weeding until established. After that, add a layer of organic mulch to help conserve water and suppress weeds [see Mulching, pg. 73]. You'll enjoy a planting that looks good year-round and requires little care. For unity of design, limit plantings to a few species. Determine the correct spacing for your plants. Measure the total area to be covered and compute the number of plants you'll need. To plant ground covers from nursery containers, follow these steps:

**1** Prepare the planting area. Rake and level the soil, adding compost in a layer 1–2 in. (25–50 mm) deep and working it in. Remove any rocks and debris from the bed.

**2** Mark each planting point based on your garden plan. Dig holes as deep as the growing container, and slightly wider.

**3** Remove plants from the nursery container. Set the plants in the holes so their root crowns are even with the surrounding soil surface. Fill the holes, using your hands to gently firm the soil.

**4** Water thoroughly, using a garden hose and sprinkler or an irrigation system. Water regularly until the plants are established.

**5** Add a rich layer of organic mulch 2–3 in. (50–75 mm) deep around the plants, away from individual stems.

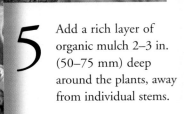

## PLANTING FERNS

**G**ive your ferns a boost by amending your planting holes with organic matter such as compost [see Establishing Planting Areas, pg. 46] and by mulching yearly with an organic mulch [see Mulching, pg. 73]. In the spring, watch for the delicate shoots called fiddleheads emerging from the soil. Within a few weeks, they will unfold to feathery fronds. With a little special care, ferns are easy to plant and grow. To plant a fern from a large nursery container, follow these steps:

**1** Prepare the bed and gently invert the plant, supporting it. Flex the container to remove the fern, taking care to avoid damaging its fronds or roots.

**2** Mark the planting point based on your garden plan. Dig a planting hole as wide and 2 in. (50 mm) deeper than the container. Add approximately 2 in. (50 mm) of organic matter to the hole.

**3** Place the fern in the hole, positioning it so the top of the root mass is slightly above the surrounding soil surface. Add or remove soil to level the plant.

**4** Fill the hole, mounding soil up to the root crown. Firm the soil with the open palms of your hands.

**5** Add a layer of organic mulch 2–3 in. (50–100 mm) thick around the base of the fern, 3 in. (75 mm) away from the crown.

**6** Water thoroughly, using a watering can or a garden hose with a diffusing nozzle. Water regularly until the fern is established.

## NATURAL GARDEN BULBS

Crocuses, daffodils, tulips, snowdrops—bulbs are the essence of spring to many people. Bulbs are plants that store everything they need to flower underground—usually in a true bulb, but sometimes in other structures variously called corms, tubers, and rhizomes. In general usage, all these structures are called bulbs.

Bulbs are tough, adaptable, and often drought-tolerant. They add extra color with minimal effort. Bulbs are superb for use as companion plants to perennials, ground covers, ferns, and ornamental grasses, and are a welcome addition to cottage, woodland, prairie, meadow, coastal, and wetland gardens [see Encyclopedia of Natural Garden Plants, pg. 94].

Many bulbs have the ability to naturalize—to spread and return, year after year, in greater numbers. Naturalizing describes how, in ideal conditions, plants will thrive and spread unassisted to become part of the natural landscape. Some bulbs naturalize by multiplying underground and forming offsets that will grow into blooming plants. Other bulbs spread by seed; they self-sow after blooming. If you want bulbs to naturalize in your garden, allow the blooms to remain until they completely fade and allow bulb foliage to fully mature. Flowers, leaves, and stems should be yellow and withered before removal. This permits the flowers to scatter their seeds and the leaves to produce nutrients that will help to stock the bulb with energy for the next year's flower display.

Bulbs flourish in every region. Choose bulbs suited to your plant hardiness zone, soil, and site conditions and they will thrive with little care and usually without fertilizer. Some bulbs will survive only if they experience an extended period of chilling cold. Good drainage is also important for long-term survival.

Plant spring-flowering bulbs in September or October in most cold-winter zones, several weeks before the soil freezes. Plant summer-blooming bulbs in early spring. Find bulbs at direct merchants, nurseries, and garden centers. They are shipped from the grower at the proper planting time for your area. In stores, examine bulbs for mold, soft spots, or other signs of distress. Avoid bulbs that have been collected from the wild, and select first-quality bulbs.

*Naturalized narcissus greet spring in a joyful burst of color that takes just weeks to develop from sprout to bloom. With proper care, each year the display will increase in beauty as the bulbs divide and produce offset plants.*

*Bulb planters are invaluable tools for planting bulbs, corms, and tubers. Choose one that is made of sturdy metal. The cutting edge will penetrate both turf and the soil beneath, creating a perfect planting hole every time for your bulbs.*

## PLANTING BULBS

**R**eplicate nature's patterns for the best effect when planting bulbs. Layer large and small bulbs together and plant odd numbers of bulbs randomly. Dig curving trenches and stagger bulbs within the trench to create drifts. Generally, dig holes 3–4 times as deep as the height of the bulb and 2–3 times the diameter of the bulb. Gather together a narrow trowel, border spade, or bulb planter and a measuring stick, and follow these steps:

**1** Prepare the planting area. Dig holes or curved trenches to proper depth and width. Loosen the soil at the bottom of the hole. In turfgrass areas, use a planting tool to dig holes.

**2** Mix organic compost with native soil only if the soil in the planting area is too compacted, amending the soil in each planting hole as the bulb is set in place. Most bulb plantings require little fertilizer or amendments.

**3** Space bulbs according to type. Set each bulb into its hole, root end down, pointed end up. If you are planting tubers or corms, place them with their immature sprouts up. Sometimes the orientation of the tuber or corm is unclear—if so, plant them on their side.

**4** Loosely pack soil around bulbs, eliminating air pockets. Fill the hole with soil. Water thoroughly after planting and whenever the soil has dried.

## PERENNIAL FLOWERS

*(Top) Orange coneflowers bloom in striking color, followed by later development of ornamental seed heads. The perennial is closely related to the popular annual, black-eyed Susan.*

*(Above) Purple coneflowers come in shades of purple and red.*

*(Right) Even perennial plants prized for their foliage, such as this plantain lily, bear blooms of grace and beauty for a short time during summer.*

Perennials—plants that grow, bloom, often disappear in winter, and then reappear each spring—are essential in the creation of a natural garden. Perennial plants occur in all climates and habitats as part of nature's layered planting pattern. Perennials play an important role in every natural garden theme [see Encyclopedia of Natural Garden Plants, pg. 84].

Perennials grow in many forms, from low, creeping mats to tall, vertical spires. There are evergreen and deciduous perennial shrubs, perennials selected for their beautiful blooms, and perennials chosen for their distinctive foliage. Perennials tolerate varied conditions, from full sun to full shade, from sandy to clay soil, and from well-drained to wetland sites. Generally, use perennials to fill the middle space in your planting design, below the trees and shrubs and above ground covers. Perennials also are effective as border and bedding plants, in masses, and as accent plants.

Flowering perennials bloom for a set amount of time—usually 2–6 weeks. To ensure your garden looks its best all season long, look for perennials with long blooming periods and attractive foliage.

Native plants will echo your natural surroundings, but keep in mind there are many plants native to other regions that also will thrive at your site. Note that portions of the foliage or flowers of some perennials can bear toxic compounds, which are hazardous if touched or eaten. Always observe caution if your garden will be visited by children or pets.

All nurseries, garden centers, and direct merchants carry a range of perennials during planting seasons. Also seek out specialty retailers for particular purposes—local natives, plants that attract birds or butterflies, or unique cultivars that suit your design. Perennials are available as bare-root divisions, field-grown clumps, and in various sizes of nursery containers. Larger sizes give you a quicker result, smaller are more economical. With the right care, all will make a smooth transition to your garden.

## PLANTING PERENNIALS

**1** Remove the plant from the nursery container. Gently loosen its rootball.

Give your perennials a good start and they'll return to delight you each year. Midspring is the best planting time for cold-winter climates; in regions with mild winters, autumn or early spring can be better. Your plants need a chance to develop roots before they experience the stress of extreme temperatures. You may plant container-grown perennials throughout the growing season, as long as you provide adequate water. Add a layer of organic mulch around plants to help conserve water and control weeds [see Mulching, pg. 73]. To plant perennials from large nursery containers, follow these steps:

**2** Space plants in the bed. Dig holes as deep as the container and one-third wider.

**3** Set the plant in the hole so that its root crown is level with the surrounding soil surface and matches the soil level of the container. Fill the hole, using your hands to gently firm the soil around the stem.

**4** Water the base of the plant thoroughly using a watering can with a diffusing rose. Water regularly thereafter until it is established.

**5** Add mulch around the base of the plant in a layer 2–3-in. (50–75-mm) deep, 1–2 in. (25–50 mm) away from the stem.

**6** Protect the plants from drying wind and sun until established. Use filter fabric, umbrellas, or cardboard boxes to shadow each plant, as needed.

## SHRUBS

Shrubs serve as the backbone of many gardens. They create screens, help define spaces, and provide the walls and middle layers of many planting designs. Shrubs provide form, texture, and color in the landscape as well as providing food and shelter for migrating and resident birds.

Shrubs grow in a wide variety of forms, from spreading mounds less than 2 feet (60 cm) tall, to sizes that match many trees. Evergreen shrubs offer foliage in many colors; deciduous shrubs also provide seasonal colors. Many flowering shrubs burst into fragrant flower early in spring, a welcome sight that also helps extend a garden's blooming season.

Another appealing aspect of shrubs in the natural garden is the fruits and berries many produce. These colorful garden additions provide visual interest and food for visiting birds.

There are shrubs for most any soil and growing condition: sandy and clay soil, sun and shade areas, wet and dry sites. Once established, many shrubs are drought-tolerant. Choose shrubs that meet your plant hardiness, soil type, and site conditions and that also suit your natural garden theme [see Encyclopedia of Natural Garden Plants, pg. 98]. Choose carefully; shrubs are permanent plants that will have a place in your garden for many years.

Always consider a shrub's mature height and width—its size when full grown. Most shrubs need roughly 10 years to reach maturity. Planning placement with ultimate size in mind will reduce considerably your need for pruning, as well as avoid any future need to move the plants in the face of over-crowding. When you do prune, accentuate the shrub's natural shape, avoiding geometric forms. Topiary is lovely, yet rarely is found in nature or a natural garden.

Generally, shrubs are available in one of three forms: containerized, bare root, or ball-and-burlap. The majority of shrubs are planted from plastic containers in sizes from 2 quarts to 10 gallons (2–38 l). Bare-root plants are shipped while dormant and need immediate attention and planting. Ball-and-burlap wrapped plants are larger and provide immediate effect.

*Asked to name natural shrubs, most western gardeners will immediately think of azalea and rhododendron, two Pacific coastal resident plants that also are found in gardens throughout nearly every region and locale.*

## PLANTING
## CONTAINER SHRUBS

**1** Prepare the planting area. Mark each planting point based on your garden plan. Dig the planting hole as deep as the container and at least twice as wide.

The best times for planting shrubs in most regions are spring and autumn, when temperatures are cooler. With careful watering, and depending on spring and summer temperatures in your zone, container-grown shrubs can be planted at any time during the growing season. Use correct shrub planting techniques—watering new plants regularly until they are established—to ensure their ultimate success. Add a layer of organic mulch around shrubs to help conserve water and control weeds [see Mulching, pg. 73]. Large shrubs planted in windy sites may require support by staking. To plant a container shrub, follow these steps:

**2** Remove the shrub from the container and lay it on its side. Loosen the root mass, untangling encircling roots.

**3** Set the shrub in the hole so that the base of the shrub is even with the surrounding soil surface and matches the soil level of the container. Spread the roots into the extra width.

**4** Fill the hole, holding the shrub to maintain its placement and using your hands to gently firm the soil around the base. Water to settle the soil, adding more as needed.

**5** Create a watering moat around the base of the shrub. Fill the moat with water at least twice after planting to saturate thoroughly. Water regularly until established.

**6** Add mulch around the shrub's base in a layer 2–4-in. (5–10-cm) thick, keeping clear an area 4–6 in. (10–15 cm) away from the shrub's stem or trunk.

## TREES

A landscape tree is a long-term investment that promises great returns. Before you install any tree, learn all you can about it. Choose only trees suited to your plant hardiness zone, soil type, and site conditions. Pick one resistant to pests and diseases. Confirm the mature size of the tree and consider its scale to your garden and home. Imagine it in your natural garden theme [see Encyclopedia of Natural Garden Plants, pg. 104].

*Planting trees is for those with patience. The rule "a year to sleep, a year to creep, and a year to leap" applies to many trees, signifying that transplant shock slows growth for several seasons before real growth begins. For slow-growing species, it may require decades before the tree assumes its mature height.*

Locate any tree a sufficient distance from your home to allow for full growth. Avoid planting tall trees under overhead utility wires. Verify the way the tree's roots grow: Most roots naturally grow in a spreading pattern. Some trees have shallow roots capable of cracking nearby pavement; locate these trees away from paved surfaces such as a patio or sidewalk. Other tree roots grow very deep; avoid these trees if underground utility and sewer lines are nearby.

Trees are commonly available in four forms: bare root, ball-and-burlapped, container plants, and spaded trees. Bare-root trees require immediate planting and are economical. Ball-and-burlapped trees are dug from the ground with a ball of soil surrounding the roots. Container trees, grown in plastic pots or wooden boxes above ground, are increasingly popular and are available in a wide range of sizes, from small to very large specimens. Spaded trees are often full-grown specimens offered by specialty nurseries.

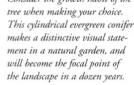

*Consider the growth habit of the tree when making your choice. This cylindrical evergreen conifer makes a distinctive visual statement in a natural garden, and will become the focal point of the landscape in a dozen years.*

There are trade-offs when choosing trees of various sizes. Large landscape trees may take three to five years to settle in; you'll find that smaller trees will become established more quickly and grow faster. If you want immediate visual impact, go with a large specimen. For economy, choose small trees, which eventually may grow to surpass the larger trees in size. To plant the largest specimen trees, seek aid from a landscape contractor that specializes in such work.

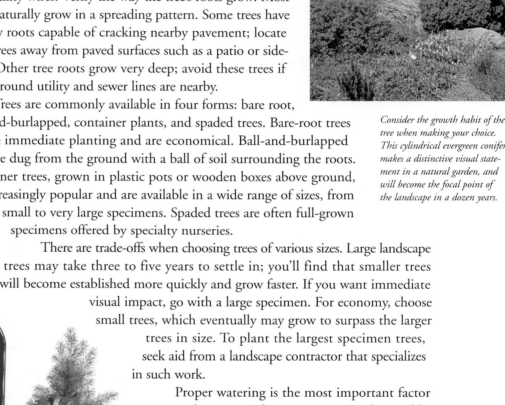

Proper watering is the most important factor to a tree's success. Always water a tree thoroughly at planting and regularly until it is well established, typically several years. Water trees deeply to produce an extensive network of roots well below the surface. Proper watering will cause trees to grow extensive root systems that can absorb water from deep in the soil rather than an unnaturally shallow root system seeking surface water. In most regions, it is best to water established trees only in drought. If you live in an arid climate, plan to deep water your established landscape trees every 2 weeks.

## PLANTING LARGE TREES

**P**lant most trees in spring or autumn, when temperatures are moderate. Some trees transplant well only in spring; ask your nursery professional for advice. In most situations, set the trunk flare—the base of the tree where the trunk enters the root ball—level or slightly above the surrounding soil. In poorly drained clay soil, position about one-third of the root ball above the surface soil and taper covering soil to ground level. Add a layer of organic mulch around trees to help conserve water and control weeds [see Mulching, pg. 73]. Stake trees in windy sites. To plant a ball-and-burlapped tree in loam, follow these steps:

1 Prepare the planting area. Mark each planting point based on your garden plan. Dig a saucer-shaped planting hole as deep as the root ball and 2–3 times as wide.

2 Set the tree in the hole. Align the trunk flare with the soil surface. Untie, pull back, and cut away burlap from upper one-third of the ball. Remove synthetic burlap completely.

3 Fill the hole two-thirds full. Water to settle the soil and eliminate air, then backfill. Form a moat outside the perimeter of the root ball.

4 Water thoroughly, using a garden hose, at the rate of soil absorption for 30 minutes. Water regularly until the tree is established.

5 Spread a ring of organic mulch 2–4 in. (50–100 mm) deep in a circle 4–6 in. (10–15 cm) away from the tree's trunk.

6 If necessary, add wooden support stakes on each side of the tree. Nail rubber ties to the stakes and loosely wrap the ties around the trunk in a figure-8 pattern, allowing the tree limited movement.

## WATER GARDEN PLANTS

*(Above) Water garden features can be created within the theme of a natural garden. Here, a stump was hollowed and lined to create a planting basin.*

*(Bottom) Tropical plants, here canna lily (inset), broadleaf philodendron, and amaryllis, are well-suited for planting near water features.*

Natural appearing water features—ponds, streams, waterfalls, and wetlands—whether existing or built, portable or permanent, present possibilities for the cultivation of specialized plants that thrive in wet sites.

Water lilies are one family of plants that immediately come to mind when contemplating a water garden. These and other aquatic plants, growing in and around water features, soften hard edges of structural features, help blend the water feature into the surrounding landscape, filter the water, and provide cover for fish.

There are four categories of aquatic plants. Shoreline plants grow in the moist soil around the edges of the water, marginals and deep-water submersible plants grow in soil in the water, and floaters grow atop or within the water. Plant shoreline plants directly in the soil outside the liner of a water feature. Plant marginals and deep-water submersible plants in suitable growing medium within a specialized container—a shallow plastic basket or porous terra-cotta pot. Then place the container in the water to the depth required for the plant. Generally, shallow-depth marginals grow in water less than 6 inches (15 cm) deep, deep-depth marginals grow in water 6–12 inches (15–30 cm) deep, and deep-water submersibles grow deeper than 12 inches (30 cm) underwater. Use supports to adjust the depth of the baskets, removing the baskets from the water for care.

Surface floaters grow unanchored by floating on the top of the water, while submerged oxygenators grow below the surface. Place them in the water to grow, tethering them with monofilament line to hold their position. Many floating plants have a tendency to spread and require frequent thinning. A few, like water hyacinth, have attained weedlike nuisance status. Most aggressive plants are prohibited.

## PLANTING AQUATIC PLANTS

**I**n nature, aquatic plants grow directly in saturated soil. In a garden setting it's much easier to grow the plants in specialized containers placed in the water rather than planting them in soil within the feature's liner. This makes it easy to remove the container and plants from the water for routine maintenance and care. Weight containers with a base of rock under the soil, and coat them with pea gravel to prevent water from washing away the planting soil. To plant submerged aquatic plants in a self-contained water garden, pond, or wetland, follow these steps:

**1** Choose an appropriate aquatic planting container and growing medium suited to the plant. Line the container with landscaping filter fabric.

**2** Fill the planter with growing medium to 2 in. (50 mm) below its rim. Leave a hole the same size as the nursery container. Remove the plant from the nursery container.

**3** Set the plant in the planter. Position its growth bud 1–2 in. (25–50 mm) above the growing medium. Using your hands, firm the growing medium around the plant.

**4** Cover the growing medium to the rim of the container with small-diameter gravel. It will protect the plant's roots and surrounding soil from erosion.

**5** Position the container at the required depth within the water feature. Use rocks to anchor the container in position, firmly holding it.

## ARID CLIMATE PLANTS

A surprisingly diverse range of plants has developed survival strategies to thrive in desert and arid regions. Small deciduous trees drop their leaves to conserve fluids when water is scarce. Succulents have waxy coatings to slow water loss and an internal system for water storage. When rain does fall, annuals germinate, grow, and bloom quickly, while shrubs and perennials burst into bloom to take advantage of the moisture.

Most desert gardens feature succulents that provide strong architectural forms around which you can plant drought-tolerant shrubs, perennials, and wildflowers. Arid gardens receive more rainfall than desert gardens, can sustain a greater choice of plants, and appear more lush. Arid conditions vary across a mountainous swath of the North American west. Design ideas include cottage and woodland gardens to themes reflective of the regional landscape.

For natural gardens in arid regions, select drought-tolerant plants well adapted to your climate. Elevation, soil type, and rainfall quantity and timing all combine to determine the specific types of plants that will thrive in your garden. Seek out tough native plants, as well as plants from other hot and dry areas of the globe.

Remember the principles of xeriscape [see Desert and Arid Gardens, pg. 7] when designing your garden and choosing plants. Group plants with similar water needs together. Although all your plants should be drought tolerant, drip irrigation will allow you to sustain plant growth, prolong the flowering, and increase the variety of plants you can grow. Plants that need more water can be planted in swales to take advantage of natural drainage patterns. Take advantage of slower water evaporation by planting in areas next to walls or beneath shade structures.

Local nurseries are a great resource for the specific knowledge it takes to plan and plant a desert or arid garden.

*When infrequent thunderstorm downpours supply them with water, dryland trees erupt in spectacular bloom.*

*Mix sun-loving perennials with arid-garden favorites to create gardens with surprising color. Cactus and succulents bloom with dramatic flowers, as do other desert dwelling plants. Here, drought-resistant ice plant plays off a succulent, aloe.*

## PLANTING A CACTUS

**1** Prepare the planting area. Mark the planting point based on your garden plan.

**W**hen planting cacti, avoid hazard by protecting yourself from spines: wear long sleeves and protective gloves. Check individual water requirements for the particular cactus being planted. Some species benefit from water applied shortly after planting, while others require a resting period for damaged roots to form protective calluses. In the desert and arid garden, small-diameter gravel serves the same purpose as organic mulch in other gardens, conserving water and suppressing weeds [see Mulching, pg. 73]. To plant most cacti, follow these general steps:

**2** Dig a planting hole as deep as the nursery container and slightly wider.

**3** Using shears, carefully cut away the nursery container and position the cactus in the hole, matching its soil level to that of the nursery container. Wear gloves to avoid abrasions.

**4** Fill the hole with soil. Using the back of a hand trowel while wearing gloves to avoid sharp thorns, tamp soil to fill all voids and settle the cactus.

**5** If recommended for the species, water. Spread small-diameter gravel as a mulch around the base of the plant.

B ecause you've chosen plants appropriate for your plant hardiness zone, soil type, and site conditions, you've helped ensure healthy, long-lived plants and a garden that is easy to tend.

This chapter describes how to make your natural garden flourish: watering, fertilizing, mulching, pruning, and controlling pests and diseases. Give your garden extra attention for the first few years while its plants become established. Once your garden is mature, care is minimal. Simple seasonal care will become part of the pattern of your year.

Watering and weeding are especially important while your new plants are growing roots and adjusting to their surroundings. Use an automatic irrigation system to save effort and water. Weeds compete with your plants for water and nutrients. Pulling weed stems and roots by hand is the most natural weeding method. Remember that some so-called weeds are plant volunteers that should be welcomed in your garden. Use care to identify new seedlings as weed or wildflower before removing them. Most gardens benefit from an ample layer of mulch to conserve water, suppress weeds, and supply nutrients to the soil. Additional fertilizing may be needed to supply nutrients missing from your soil.

Though natural-style garden landscapes usually require less pruning, you still will need to guide the growth of woody plants and keep your garden tidy by dead-heading spent blooms from perennials and annuals.

As caretaker, it pays to be observant of your natural garden. Keep an eye on it, dealing with conditions before they become difficult to control. Note signs of water stress, insect invasion, and disease, and decide on the best courses of action. Consider the approach of environmentally friendly gardening and manage weeds, pests, and disease without garden chemicals [see Beautiful Natural Gardens, pg. 1].

Finally, understand that caring for a garden is a pleasant activity—healthy and productive.

> **Once established natural gardens are carefree, compared to many more traditional garden designs**

# Caring for Natural Gardens

*Natural gardens with native plants and plants that are well-adapted to your climate zone require a minimum of care. Cleanup of winter debris from the beds is a springtime task.*

## WATERING AND FERTILIZING

With proper plant selection, a natural garden will flourish while conserving water. Still, irrigation is essential at times. New plantings are especially vulnerable to drought stress. Plants absorb water through their roots; new plants must grow roots before they can meet their water needs. With trees and shrubs, plan for two years of careful watering; with perennials, grasses, and ground covers, care through the first growing season is sufficient in most regions.

*Use a rain gauge to measure how much water nature provides; they are available at most nurseries and garden centers.*

Watering during drought conditions—when rainfall is below average or entirely absent—will increase the health of your garden. To identify drought stress, look for wilting or browning foliage. Investigate by digging a hole into the soil with a narrow trowel; if the top 3 inches (75 mm) of soil are dry, you should water.

When you water, soak the soil deeply to encourage deep root growth. Verify the watering needs of specific plants. Water thoroughly and allow the soil to dry between waterings to create natural drought resistance in many plants. Remember, plants that require moist soil need more frequent attention.

Match your watering methods to your needs and your garden size. In small gardens a hose with a watering wand or watering cans may be sufficient. In larger spaces, consider using soaker hoses or try an automatic drip irrigation system [see Installing In-Ground Irrigation, pg. 42]. Study the water spray pattern of overhead sprinklers and carefully place them to conserve water and reduce potential runoff.

Choose plants well adapted to your soil, reducing or possibly even eliminating the need for fertilizing. In nature, plants receive the nutrients they need from the soil as part of a natural cycle. Overfertilization promotes soft growth that invites pests and harbors disease. Meet your plant's nutrient needs by adding organic matter or a mulch [see Mulching, opposite].

When you fertilize, organic fertilizers are always best for your plants and the environment. Synthetic fertilizers lack many trace nutrients and all beneficial organisms, and may pollute waterways and groundwater. Decomposed organic fertilizers release their nutrients slowly over time, avoiding shock to plants and chemical burn.

**MULCHING**

Mulch—a protective blanket spread over the soil—is an invaluable ally to the natural garden. It benefits your plants and the environment, reducing maintenance and conserving water. Visually, a layer of mulch unifies the garden floor and sets off plants in an attractive way. Organic mulches are those made of decomposable plant material. Inorganic mulches—primarily gravel and rocks—also can be effective in the right garden setting. In arid or desert gardens, organic mulch sometimes keeps the soil too moist, leading to fungal diseases that can kill plants. For such areas, an inorganic mulch works best.

Mulch conserves water. A generous layer of mulch seals in moisture, prevents evaporation, slows water runoff and erosion, and insulates the soil from temperature changes. It helps suppress weeds, which need light to germinate.

Organic mulches act as soil conditioners. They break down slowly, adding organic matter that replenishes the soil's nutrients and helps maintain its texture.

The best type of organic mulch for your garden depends on regional suitability, cost, garden theme, and availability. Shredded leaves, shredded bark, bark chips, and pine needles are some of the possibilities. Check nearby landscape suppliers or garden centers for cocoa bean hulls, crushed corncobs, cottonseed and rice hulls, or other regionally available agricultural by-products that make suitable mulch. Some mulch materials deplete nitrogen as they decompose; you may need to lightly fertilize to counteract this tendency.

Apply a layer 1–4 inches (25–100 mm) deep around and between plants. The depth depends on the plant type and site. To help prevent pests and diseases, keep mulch away from the stems of plants and the trunks of trees.

Most mulch decomposes slowly over a period of months. Some mulches last several seasons before thinning. Whenever your initial application of mulch begins to thin or decompose, replenish it with an additional layer of mulch 1–2 inches (25–50 mm) deep. This occasional activity will save you hours of time spent watering and weeding.

## FERTILIZING NATURALLY

In nature, leaves, branches, and debris decompose to enrich and condition the soil through the action of earthworms, insects, and microorganisms. Improve your soil's condition the natural way by applying organic mulch. Mulch breaks down into humus and serves as a low-level fertilizer. A topdressing of compost can double as mulch and a natural fertilizer in gardens with high nutrient needs. Create garden compost by allowing disease-free garden clippings, vegetable scraps, and leaves to break down over time into rich soil [see Amending the Soil, pg. 47].

*Use a small rake made especially for the purpose when spreading mulch around sensitive, easily damaged plants. A layer that covers the soil completely is best, though you always should keep the mulch from touching the plant's stem or crown.*

## PRUNING

In a natural garden, you'll prune selectively to enhance a plant's natural shape and promote its overall health.

Some shrubs need pruning to remove old growth and encourage young vigorous new growth. Some shrubs and trees need thinning to remove any twiggy growth in their center. Trees must be pruned to remove crossing branches, which grow through the tree's center, and to create a balanced framework. Pruning is especially important in newly planted shade trees. Creating a sound structure early on will shape the tree's future growth in the right direction.

Consider the mature size of trees and shrubs before you plant. Avoid using pruning as a method to keep a large plant small.

Improve the health of all trees and shrubs by removing the three D's: dead, diseased, or damaged branches. When removing diseased branches, always cut to healthy wood nearer the stem. Afterwards, disinfect your pruning or lopping shears using a mixture of one part household bleach to nine parts water, to avoid spreading infections to other plants. Remember to wear gloves and protect your clothing when using bleach.

Keep your pruning tools sharp. Sharp blades avoid crushing stems and tearing bark. Use long-handled loppers or a pruning saw for branches too large to be easily severed with bypass pruning shears. When removing tree branches, cut outside the branch collar—a series of ridges at the limb's junction with the trunk. Cut large branches with two separate cuts of the saw. Make the undercut first, beginning near the tree trunk and cutting halfway through the branch. Follow with a cut made farther out from the trunk and down from the top. Cutting like this avoids skinning bark from the trunk as the limb falls. To avoid hazards, always consult an arborist when removing large limbs, taking down trees, or cutting branches near power lines.

*Use a telescoping pole pruner to cut tall overhead trees. The tool has a bypass shear for twigs and small branches and a pruning saw for thicker limbs. Remember that pruning overhead may cause hazard from falling branches; always wear protective headgear, safety glasses, and gloves when using a pole pruner.*

## DEADHEADING

Deadheading—removing faded flowers—is a gardening technique as opposed to a rock-and-roll lifestyle.

Deadheading annuals and perennials often encourages the production of more flowers, prevents self-sowing, and keeps your garden fresh and tidy. To deadhead, pinch off the fading flower heads and their stalks using the nails of your thumb and forefinger or sharp bypass pruning shears. Leave some of the fading blooms that produce attractive seedpods to provide food for birds and add visual interest. Allow seed to form if you wish to have your flowers self-sow, creating new volunteer plants that add to the charm of your garden in following seasons. Deadhead each time you visit your garden, making it part of your routine.

## PRUNING SHRUBS

Periodically prune shrubs to accentuate their form and help keep them free of disease. Pruning suckering shrubs also invigorates their growth. Use sharp bypass pruning shears to make clean cuts. Examine plants annually to determine if pruning is needed. To prune a shrub with a treelike branching pattern, follow these steps:

**1** To start, remove wayward branches that deviate from the shrub's natural form. Cut them back to lateral branches.

**2** Annual growth spikes top many woody shrubs. Cut them 4–6 in. (10–15 cm) below the prior year's growth margin. Retain natural branching forms.

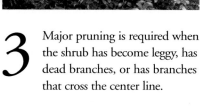

**3** Major pruning is required when the shrub has become leggy, has dead branches, or has branches that cross the center line.

**4** Prune away crossing branches at the trunk. Choose the weakest branches to remove first, then progress to larger limbs.

**5** Cut to an outward-facing bud at a 45° angle about ¼ in. (6 mm) beyond the bud.

**6** Pruning allows all parts of the shrub to receive light penetration and air circulation.

## PESTS AND DISEASES

A garden habitat contains plants, animals, birds, insects, fungi, and bacteria, among others. Insects and microorganisms belong in the garden; it's only when organisms are out of balance that you should take corrective measures.

Good gardening practices are your first line of defense. A diverse group of plants helps create a pest-resistant garden. The broader your plant list, the more likely your garden will resist pests. Choose plants suited to your soil and site, and either naturally or through breeding resistant to pests and disease. Space plants properly within your design. Meet your plants' water and nutrition needs. Just as in humans, stress can make a plant vulnerable to disease.

Plants in good health still may fall ill or become infested. A natural approach to controlling pests focuses on early recognition, managing their numbers, and limiting their damage. First, learn to identify the pest and recognize signs of their damage. Books, garden center staff, and your USDA or Agriculture Canada extension can help you.

Monitor pest levels and recognize that a certain amount of damage is acceptable. A few chewed leaves are a fair trade-off for a chemical-free garden. Environmentally friendly gardening practices—manual picking, water sprays, and organic pest control—offer the best control options. Remove Japanese beetles, snails, and slugs by hand. Spray aphids and spider mites with water.

Make an ally of your pest's natural enemies. Beneficial insects are available from many garden retailers or insect supply houses for release in your garden. Remember toads, frogs, bats, and birds can eat a lot of insects, too! Attract beneficial organisms to your garden by providing them food and shelter.

Controlling disease is trickier. Viral diseases of plants are incurable; plants bearing them must be destroyed. Other plant diseases are caused by bacteria and fungi. Good cultural practices are important for controlling these diseases. Avoid overhead watering, which can contribute to the spread of pathogens. Remove infected plants or prune foliage. Avoid composting leaves and debris that might harbor disease. In autumn, remove debris around plants where organisms can overwinter. Always wash your hands and all tools used on an infected plant to avoid spreading the disease.

If damage due to insects or diseases become extensive, choose earth-friendly controls whenever possible: insecticidal soaps, fungicidal soaps, horticultural oils, and botanical pesticides derived from plants. These substances, though strong and effective, decompose quickly into harmless compounds. Use botanical pesticides sparingly and carefully. Though natural and organic, many are broad spectrum in nature. All pesticides may affect birds and wildlife and eliminate the beneficial insects that help keep pest populations in check. Apply them directly to the pest organism or infected foliage, avoiding broadcast spraying of the garden.

If you must resort to garden chemicals, choose one targeted to your specific pest for use on your specific plant. Follow all package instructions carefully and completely. Always wear protective clothing and properly dispose of empty containers.

*Beneficial animals, insects, and bacteria far outnumber pests in healthy gardens. Many studies reveal that more than 90 percent of all organisms are benign or helpful. The toad shown here is a good example. Frogs and toads eat hundreds of insects each day.*

## APPLYING INSECTICIDAL SOAP

**I**nsecticidal soaps are made of fatty acids that penetrate the skin of soft-bodied insects, including aphids and mites, and dissolve cell membranes. For larger insects, they control by suffocation. These soaps must contact the pest to be effective and become harmless when dry. For the best control, monitor your plants for pests and treat them when infestation is noticed. Some plants develop foliage burn in reaction to insecticidal soap; test a leaf or two before broad application. Avoid indiscriminate spraying of unaffected foliage, and follow these steps:

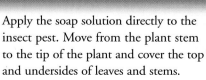

**2** Choose a control specific to your pest and that is safe for use on your plant. Test a small section of foliage before application. Read and follow exactly all package instructions when you mix and apply the control. Wear protective clothing, gloves, and eye protection.

**1** Identify the pest. Seek help by describing the pest or collecting it along with part of the damaged plant, placing the sample in a sealed plastic bag, and taking it to your garden center for assistance.

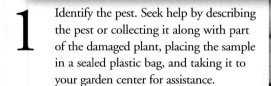

**4** Dispose of empty containers and unused solution according to package instructions. Rinse all tools, equipment, and clothing thoroughly before storing.

**3** Apply the soap solution directly to the insect pest. Move from the plant stem to the tip of the plant and cover the top and undersides of leaves and stems.

T he plant encyclopedia is designed to help you choose the right plants for your natural garden. Plants are arranged by their type: annual, perennial, bulb, shrub, tree, grass, vine, ground cover, and fern. Because the same flower may be called by various common names by region, each plant in the encyclopedia is identified by its common name and its universally recognized scientific name. Each encyclopedia entry also contains the following information:

**Description/habit:** This category gives you an idea of the plant's appearance, how it grows, and its mature size.

**Bloom color/season:** Use the photographs and the color and season of bloom information to coordinate the blooming plants within your garden and plan the garden's appearance throughout the year.

**Plant hardiness:** Use the USDA plant hardiness zones as a guideline. Consult local experts if your garden has microclimates that fall outside the zone for your area.

**Soil needs:** Every plant prefers a particular type of soil. Fertility refers to the level of nutrients that must be available in the soil for the plant to thrive. Choose plants that most closely match the soil type found in your planting area. Acid-alkaline balance is measured by pH on a scale with 7.0 as neutral. Lower numbers are acidic and higher numbers are alkaline.

**Planting:** Plants grow best when they have proper amounts of light, air, and water. Use the plant spacing guidelines to optimize plant health and to ensure that plants have enough room to grow to their mature size.

**Care:** When you choose plants, remember the plant's needs and also your own. Most plants need special attention until they are established. The watering requirements and other care described here indicate the level of long-term care required.

**Features:** This category offers suggestions on how to use the plant in a specific garden theme. It also lists special characteristics that make the plant noteworthy.

Enjoy the bounty of nature's garden with a selection of plants suited to the regional variety of the North American landscape

# Encyclopedia of Natural Garden Plants

*Plants picked carefully for your natural garden will provide lasting pleasure and beauty. Choose plants that are native to your area or those that grow best in climate and soil conditions that are similar to those found in your garden.*

## ANNUALS

**Common name:** Baby-blue-eyes
**Scientific name:** *Nemophila Menziesii*
**Description/habit:** Hardy, spreading annual, 6 in. (15 cm) tall.
Finely cut, green leaves. Flowers 1 in. (25 mm) across.
**Bloom color/season:** Blue with white centers. Spring–frost.
**Plant hardiness:** Zones 2–10.
**Soil needs:** Moist, well-drained. Fertility: Rich with humus supplement. 6.5–7.0 pH.
**Planting:** Full sun to partial shade. 6–12 in. (15–30 cm) apart. In
frost-free areas, sow seeds in autumn for early spring bloom.
**Care:** Moderate. Water in drought conditions. Propagate by seed.
**Features:** Good choice for edges in cottage, meadow gardens. North
American native.

**Common name:** Black-eyed Susan
**Scientific name:** *Rudbeckia hirta*
**Description/habit:** Upright, branching, herbaceous annual, biennial, or short-lived perennial, 2–3 ft. (60–90 cm) tall; some cultivars are shorter. Lance-shaped, rough, hairy leaves. Flowers showy, daisylike, with dark cones in center, 2–4 in. (50–100 mm) across, even up to 7 in. (18 cm).
**Bloom color/season:** Orange-yellow blend with black center. Summer–autumn.
**Plant hardiness:** Zones 3–10.
**Soil needs:** Well-drained, moist. Fertility: Average. 7.0 pH.
**Planting:** 1 ft. (30 cm) apart.
**Care:** Easy. Water in drought conditions. Deadhead to encourage flowering. Propagate by division, seed, cuttings.
**Features:** Good choice for borders, massing in cottage, meadow gardens. Good cut flower. Attracts butterflies. Eastern, midwestern U.S. native.

**Common name:** Cornflower; Bachelor's-button
**Scientific name:** *Centaurea Cyanus*
**Description/habit:** Upright, old-fashioned annual, 8–30 in. (20–75 cm) tall. Linear, gray-green leaves. Flowers rounded, 1–1½ in. (25–38 mm) across.
**Bloom color/season:** Blue, pink, rose, white. Spring–summer.
**Plant hardiness:** Zones 3–9.
**Soil needs:** Well-drained, sandy. Fertility: Average. 7.0 pH.
**Planting:** Full sun. 1–2 ft. (30–60 cm) apart.
**Care:** Easy. Water in drought conditions. Deadhead to encourage flowering. Propagate by seed, cuttings.
**Features:** Good choice for borders, edgings in cottage, meadow gardens. Good cut flower. Can be invasive.

**Common name:** Godetia; Farewell-to-spring; Satin Flower
**Scientific name:** *Clarkia amoena*
**Description/habit:** Upright annual, 1–3 ft. (30–90 cm) tall. Tapered, green leaves. Flowers 2–3 in. (50–75 mm) across.
**Bloom color/season:** Pink, white, red, lavender, often with darker centers. Spring–early summer.
**Plant hardiness:** Zones 2–10.
**Soil needs:** Well-drained, sandy. Fertility: Average, tolerates poor soil. 7.0 pH.
**Planting:** Full sun to partial shade. 8–10 in. (20–25 cm) apart. Sow seeds directly into soil.
**Care:** Easy. Water in drought conditions. Pinch off growing tips to encourage bushy shape. Propagate by seed.
**Features:** Good choice for beds, borders in woodland, meadow, coastal gardens. Will self-sow. Western U.S. and Canada native.

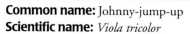

**Common name:** Johnny-jump-up
**Scientific name:** *Viola tricolor*
**Description/habit:** Short-lived, tufted perennial often grown as an annual, 6–12 in. (15–30 cm) tall. Oval, lobed, medium green leaves, 1–2 in. (25–50 mm) long. Flowers rounded, with overlapping petals, flat-faced, about 2 in. (50 mm) across.
**Bloom color/season:** Combination white/purple/yellow, the classic old-fashioned viola, also yellow/blue/purple. Late winter–early spring.
**Plant hardiness:** Zones 3–10.
**Soil needs:** Well-drained, moist. Fertility: Moderately rich. 7.0 pH.
**Planting:** Full sun to partial shade. 4–8 in. (10–20 cm) apart. Sow seeds 10–12 weeks before the last spring frost.
**Care:** Easy. Water regularly. Deadhead to encourage flowering. Propagate by division, seed, runners, offsets.
**Features:** Good choice for borders, containers, edgings, ground cover in cottage, meadow, small-space gardens. Will self-sow. European native naturalized throughout North America.

**Common name:** Love-in-a-mist
**Scientific name:** *Nigella damascena*
**Description/habit:** Upright, herbaceous annual, 18 in. (45 cm) tall. Fine-textured leaves. Single flowers 1½ in. (38 mm) across.
**Bloom color/season:** Blue, white, pink. Spring–summer.
**Plant hardiness:** Zones 2–10.
**Soil needs:** Well-drained, dry. Fertility: Average. 7.0 pH.
**Planting:** Full sun. 6–8 in. (15–20 cm) apart. Plant seeds directly in soil in an area with good air circulation.
**Care:** Easy. Water in drought conditions. Propagate by seed.
**Features:** Good choice for cottage, meadow gardens. Will self-sow. Seed pods are attractive in dried arrangements.

**Common name:** Poppy, California
**Scientific name:** *Eschscholzia californica*
**Description/habit:** Bushy perennial with many hybrids, grown as annual outside California and coastal Oregon, its native area. Fernlike, gray green leaves. Flowers cup-shaped, with 4 satiny petals, 2 in. (50 mm) across; closed at night and on gray days.
**Bloom color/season:** Gold, red, yellow, white. Spring–fall.
**Plant hardiness:** Zones 8–10 as perennial; 3–7 as annual.
**Soil needs:** Well-drained, sandy. Fertility: Average. 7.0 pH.
**Planting:** Full sun. 6 in. (15 cm) apart. Plant seeds directly in soil in autumn for early spring bloom.
**Care:** Moderate. Water moderately in drought conditions. Propagate by seed.
**Features:** Good choice for containers, edgings, hillsides, mixed borders in cottage, meadow, coastal, desert gardens. Will self-sow. Western North American native.

**Common name:** Poppy
**Scientific name:** *Papaver* species

**Warning**

Seeds of poppies are harmful if ingested. Avoid planting in gardens frequented by children or pets.

**Description/habit:** About 50 species of annuals and perennials with milk sap. Lobed, blue green leaves. Single, nodding, showy flower, usually on a long stem.
**Bloom color/season:** Red, white, violet, yellow. Spring–early summer.
**Plant hardiness:** Zones 2–10.
**Soil needs:** Well-drained. Fertility: Average. 6.5–7.0 pH.
**Planting:** Full sun. 12 in. (30 cm) apart. Sow seeds directly into soil before the last frost date.
**Care:** Easy. Water to keep soil slightly moist. Deadhead to encourage flowering. Propagate by seed.
**Features:** Good choice for borders, massing in cottage, meadow, arid gardens. Will self-sow. Some western North American natives.

**Common name:** Sage, Scarlet
**Scientific name:** *Salvia splendens*
**Description/habit:** Upright, bushy, short-lived perennial grown as annual, 1–2 ft. (30–60 cm) tall, 10–12 in. (25–30 cm) wide. Oval or lance-shaped, medium to dark green leaves. Flowers tubular, two-lipped on dense spikes.
**Bloom color/season:** Red, white, pink, mauve. Summer.
**Plant hardiness:** Zones 5–9 as perennial; 3–4 as annual.
**Soil needs:** Moist, well-drained soil. Fertility: Rich. 7.0 pH.
**Planting:** Full sun to partial shade. 1 ft. (30 cm) apart. Plant light-colored flowers in partial shade for best effect.
**Care:** Easy. Water in drought conditions. Propagate by seed.
**Features:** Good choice for accents, borders in cottage, woodland, coastal gardens. Attracts bees, hummingbirds.

## SAGE

There are hundreds of sage species, varieties, and cultivars available today. Known botanically as *Salvia*, all are members of the Mint family, a diverse genus that contains both annuals and perennials. They grow as shrubs, edging plants, and ground covers. The culinary versions are a mainstay of the kitchen or *potager* garden. All have two-lipped flowers growing in whorled patterns around spikes, and most have fragrant leaves. Sage foliage is variously narrowly oblong or broadly oval, smooth or hairy, woolly, quilted, notched, toothed, or scalloped.

Grow sage as a perennial in zones 5–9 and as an annual in zones 3–4, depending on species and your plant hardiness zone [see USDA Plant Hardiness Around the World, pg. 116]. Provide average, well-drained soil with neutral to alkaline pH, and water regularly, allowing the soil to dry completely between waterings. They need full sun, and some do quite well in dry, rocky soil. There's a place for a sage in borders, containers, or herb gardens. They're ideal for woodlands. Bees and hummingbirds find sage attractive.

Widely available scarlet sage, *S. splendens*, and mealy-cup sage, *S. farinacea*, or varieties derived from them, are long-flowering plants for borders and cottage gardens, grown as summer annuals. Bright red is the typical color of the scarlet sage, although it also is available in white, pink, and mauve. Mealy-cup sage can be found with blue and white blooms.

Bog sage, *S. uliginosa*, is a clumping perennial that grows up to 6 ft. (1.8 m) tall. Its small blue and white flowers appear in late summer and early autumn and appeal to hummingbirds. *S. officinalis* is the culinary herb often used to flavor poultry, pork, eggs, and vegetables. The leaves of 'Tricolor' are patterned with dark green, cream, and a rosy blush. 'Berggarten' has oval, quilted leaves of soft green and is flowerless.

Mexican bush sage, *S. leucantha*, is an evergreen shrub that grows 4 ft. (1.2 m) tall by 3 ft. (90 cm) wide, with linear, gray green, downy leaves on arching stems. Purple and white flowers bloom on tall spikes all summer. It's best to cut it to the ground in winter to control growth.

**Common name:** Treasure Flower
**Scientific name:** *Gazania rigens*
**Description/habit:** Many hybrids of spreading annuals to 18 in. (45 cm) tall. Narrow, silvery green leaves, silky white underneath. Flowers daisylike, 3–4 in. (75–100 mm) across, with dark centers.
**Bloom color/season:** Orange, yellow. Spring–summer.
**Plant hardiness:** Zones 7–9.
**Soil needs:** Well-drained. Fertility: Average. 7.0 pH.
**Planting:** Full sun. 18 in. (45 cm) apart.
**Care:** Easy. Water only in drought conditions. Avoid overwatering. Root rot, mildew susceptible. Propagate by division, cuttings, seed.
**Features:** Good choice for banks, containers, edgings, ground cover, hanging baskets, walls in cottage, coastal, desert gardens. Blooms close at night. Heat-, drought-, wind-tolerant.

## PERENNIALS

**Common name:** Aloe
**Scientific name:** *Aloe* species
**Description/habit:** Between 200 and 250 species of tender, long-lived, succulent perennials. Mostly stemless rosettes, some climbing. From 6–144 in. (15–360 cm) tall. Long, tapering, fleshy, green, blue green, gray green leaves, some are spiny along edges. Flowers tubular, on long, branched spikes; produced only in warm climates.
**Bloom color/season:** Orange, yellow, red, cream. Intermittently spring–fall.
**Plant hardiness:** Zones 9–10.
**Soil needs:** Well-drained, dry. Fertility: Average. 7.0 pH.
**Planting:** Full sun. 1 ft. (30 cm) apart or more, depending on species.
**Care:** Easy. Water deeply during growth; little or not at all in dormant period. Protect from frost. Propagate by suckers, cutting offsets.
**Features:** Good choice for accent, containers, edgings, rocky slopes in desert, arid gardens.

*Every soul should be put in contact with the mystery that stands stark before us but which we do not apprehend. It is in every leaf, every tender shoot, every opening flower and growing fruit, every pulse of life on the planet. The wonder of life is greater as our knowledge grows.*

LIBERTY HYDE BAILEY

**Common name:** Aster
**Scientific name:** *Aster* species
**Description/habit:** Between 200 and 500 species and named varieties of upright, branched, herbaceous herbs, perennials, biennials, and rarely annuals, 8–60 in. (20–150 cm) tall. Narrow, simple or toothed, gray, medium to dark green leaves. Flowers daisylike masses of clusters to 2 in. (50 mm) wide.
**Bloom color/season:** White, blue, purple, red, pink, lilac. Summer–fall.
**Plant hardiness:** Zones 4–9.
**Soil needs:** Well-drained, sandy. Fertility: Average to rich. 7.0 pH.
**Planting:** Full sun to partial shade. 18–36 in. (45–90 cm) apart.
**Care:** Moderate. Some are drought-tolerant. Pinch for bushy plants. May be powdery mildew susceptible in late autumn. Propagate by division, cuttings.
**Features:** Good choice for borders in cottage, woodland, meadow gardens. Good cut flowers, late-season color. Attracts butterflies. Worldwide distribution.

**Common name:** Beard-tongue
**Scientific name:** *Penstemon Digitalis*
**Description/habit:** Erect, clumping, herbaceous perennial, 2–4 ft. (60–120 cm) tall. Basal, lance-shaped leaves up to 7 in. (18 cm) long. Flowers tubular, about 1 in. (25 mm) long, on tall spikes.
**Bloom color/season:** White, light pink. Late spring–early summer.
**Plant hardiness:** Zones 3–9.
**Soil needs:** Well-drained, moist, loose. Fertility: Average. 7.0 pH.
**Planting:** Full sun to partial shade. 18–24 in. (45–60 cm) apart.
**Care:** Easy. Water regularly. Deadhead for second flowering. Propagate by seed, division in spring.
**Features:** Good choice for midheight plant for beds, borders, containers in cottage, meadow gardens. Some other *Penstemon* species grow well in arid gardens. Attracts butterflies, hummingbirds. Midwest- to Atlantic U.S. native.

**Common name:** Bee Balm; Oswego Tea
**Scientific name:** *Monarda didyma*
**Description/habit:** Upright, clumping, herbaceous perennial, 2–4 ft. (60–120 cm) tall. Mint-scented dark green leaves 4–6 in. (10–15 cm) long. Flowers whorled, long-tubed, 2 in. (50 mm) long.
**Bloom color/season:** Red, pink, lavender, salmon. Summer.
**Plant hardiness:** Zones 4–9.
**Soil needs:** Well-drained, sandy. Fertility: Average. 7.0 pH.
**Planting:** Full sun to partial shade. 10 in. (25 cm) apart. Plant in spring.
**Care:** Easy. Water to keep soil moist. Divide every few years to control spread, maintain vigor. Propagate by division.
**Features:** Good choice for foreground plant in mixed border, massing in cottage, woodland, meadow gardens. Attracts bees, butterflies, hummingbirds. Eastern U.S. native.

**Common name:** Bellflower, Willow; Peach-bells
**Scientific name:** *Campanula persicifolia*
**Description/habit:** Dainty, loose sprays of cupped single or double flowers 1½ in. (38 mm) wide. Narrow leaves 4–8 in. (10–20 cm) long. Plants grow 2–3 ft. (60–90 cm) tall. Low, slender, leafy.
**Bloom color/season:** Blue, purple, white. Spring–autumn.
**Plant hardiness:** Zones 3–10.
**Soil needs:** Well-drained. Fertility: Average. 7.0 pH.
**Planting:** Full sun to partial shade. 12–18 in. (30–45 cm) apart.
**Care:** Easy. Water regularly. Divide crowded clumps in early spring or autumn. Propagate from seed, division, cuttings.
**Features:** Good choice for borders, edgings in cottage gardens. Evergreen in warmer climates. Aster yellows susceptible

**Common name:** Bleeding-heart
**Scientific name:** *Dicentra spectabilis*
**Description/habit:** Upright, clumping perennial, short-lived in mild winter areas, 8–24 in. (20–60 cm) tall. Basal, fernlike dark blue green, gray green, or blue gray leaves. Flowers shaped like puffy hearts about 1 in. (25 mm) across, on leafless stalks, either arching or upright.
**Bloom color/season:** White, rose pink. Spring–midsummer.
**Plant hardiness:** Zones 3–9.
**Soil needs:** Well-drained, moist. Fertility: Rich. 7.0–8.0 pH.
**Planting:** Shade to partial shade. 12–18 in. (30–45 cm) apart.
**Care:** Moderate. Keep moist. Protect from wind, frost. Plants become dormant in late summer. Propagate by division, seed.
**Features:** Good choice for borders in cottage, woodland gardens. Good with ferns. Attracts butterflies. Western bleeding-heart, *D. formosa*, is a shorter species native to the Pacific northwest from California to British Columbia.

**Common name:** Bluebells, Virginia
**Scientific name:** *Mertensia virginica*
**Description/habit:** Upright, herbaceous perennial, 1–2 ft. (30–60 cm) tall. Oval, blue green leaves, 3–7 in. (75–180 mm) long. Flowers trumpetlike, drooping or nodding, in nodding clusters about 1 in. (25 mm) long.
**Bloom color/season:** Pink buds maturing to blue. Late spring.
**Plant hardiness:** Zones 3–10.
**Soil needs:** Well-drained, moist. Fertility: Rich. 6.5 pH.
**Planting:** Partial to full shade. 1 ft. (30 cm) apart.
**Care:** Easy. Keep moist during growth and bloom. Plants become dormant in early summer. Propagate by division, seed.
**Features:** Good choice for borders in cottage, woodland, wetland gardens. Good with ferns. Attracts bees. Eastern U.S. native.

**Common name:** Bluestar
**Scientific name:** *Amsonia Tabernaemontana*
**Description/habit:** Erect, clumping, hardy perennial; 2–3½ ft. (60–105 cm) tall. Willowlike, alternating leaves become bright gold in autumn. Flowers funnel-like, 5-lobed, star-shaped, ¾ in. (19 mm) across, in dainty clusters emerging in starbursts from top of plant.
**Bloom color/season:** Blue. Spring–early summer.
**Plant hardiness:** Zones 3–9.
**Soil needs:** Well-drained. Fertility: Average. 7.0 pH.
**Planting:** Full sun to partial shade. 18–24 in. (45–60 cm) apart.
**Care:** Easy. Water in drought conditions. Propagate by division, seed, cuttings.
**Features:** Good choice for accents, borders in cottage, woodland, meadow gardens. Use as frame for garden accessories. Adds textural contrast. Eastern U.S. native.

**Common name:** Columbine
**Scientific name:** *Aquilegia* species
**Description/habit:** About 70 species and many hybrids of upright, herbaceous, short-lived perennials, 1–3 ft. (30–90 cm) tall. Lacy, delicately lobed blue green leaves on branched stems. Flowers showy, nodding; 1½–2 in. (38–50 mm) wide, with 2 in. (50 mm) spurs.
**Bloom color/season:** *A. canadensis*, an eastern U.S. native, yellow with red spurs; *A. caerulea*, native of Rocky Mountains, blue with white spurs. Late spring–early summer.
**Plant hardiness:** Zones 3–9.
**Soil needs:** Well-drained, sandy, moist. Fertility: Average to rich. 7.0 pH.
**Planting:** Best in partial shade; tolerates some sun. 8–18 in. (20–45 cm) apart.
**Care:** Easy. Water regularly in dry weather, otherwise moderately. Deadhead for second flowering. Propagate by division, seed in spring.
**Features:** Good choice for borders in cottage, woodland, meadow gardens. Attracts bees, hummingbirds. Deer-resistant. Will self-sow. Northern Hemisphere native.

**Common name:** Coneflower, Purple
**Scientific name:** *Echinacea purpurea*
**Description/habit:** Erect, perennial herb, 2–4 ft. (60–120 cm) tall. Leaves 3–8 in. (75–200 mm) long, oval, dark green, coarse, toothed. Long-lasting flowers daisylike, 4 in. (10 cm) across, with drooping rays.
**Bloom color/season:** Purple with brown conical centers that remain as distinctive seed heads after petals drop. Midsummer–early autumn.
**Plant hardiness:** Zones 3–10.
**Soil needs:** Well-drained. Fertility: Average to rich. 7.0 pH.
**Planting:** Full sun. 18 in. (45 cm) apart.
**Care:** Easy. Water moderately in dry weather. Propagate by division, seed.
**Features:** Good choice for borders, massing in cottage, meadow gardens. Good cut flower. Dried seed heads are attractive. Birds eat the seeds. Attracts butterflies. Midwestern U.S. native.

**Common name:** Coralbells
**Scientific name:** *Heuchera sanguinea*
**Description/habit:** Many cultivars of dainty tufting or matting evergreen perennials, 1–2 ft. (30–60 cm) tall. Long-stalked, gray green, marbled, or purple leaves 1–2 in. (25–50 mm) wide with rounded, scalloped lobes. Flowers bell-shaped, ½ in. (13 mm) long on wiry stems to 20 in. (50 cm) tall.
**Bloom color/season:** Red, pink, white. Spring–early summer.
**Plant hardiness:** Zones 3–9.
**Soil needs:** Moist, well-drained, loam. Fertility: Average to rich. 7.0–7.5 pH.
**Planting:** Full sun to partial shade. 1 ft. (30 cm) apart. Plant in spring or autumn.
**Care:** Easy. Water regularly. Deadhead. Propagate by division, seed.
**Features:** Good choice for beds, borders, edgings in cottage, woodland gardens. Interesting foliage display. Southwestern U.S. native.

**Common name:** Coreopsis
**Scientific name:** *Coreopsis* species
**Description/habit:** Over 100 species of quite variable annuals or perennials, evergreen or deciduous. Upright or mounding, 1–3 ft. (60–90 cm) tall. Lobed or narrow, hairy or smooth, light or dark green leaves. Many single, double, or semi-double, daisylike flowers, about 2 in. (50 mm) across.
**Bloom color/season:** Orange, yellow, white, pink, maroon. Spring–autumn.
**Plant hardiness:** Zones 4–9.
**Soil needs:** Well-drained. Fertility: Poor to average. 7.0 pH.
**Planting:** Full sun. To 3 ft. (90 cm) apart, depending on species.
**Care:** Easy. Drought-tolerant, avoid overwatering. Deadhead to encourage flowering. Propagate by division, seed, cuttings.
**Features:** Good choice for borders, containers, edgings in cottage, meadow, desert gardens. Good cut flower. Attracts bees, birds, butterflies. Some will self-sow. *C. verticillata* 'Moonbeam' is popular cultivar. North American native.

**Common name:** Dusty-miller
**Scientific name:** *Senecio Cineraria*
**Description/habit:** Upright, stiff, bushy, spreading half-hardy perennial, can be grown as annual, 12–30 in. (30–75 cm) tall. Attractive woolly white leaves, in some cultivars finely cut, lacy; in others broad, lobed, toothed. Flowers daisylike in terminal clusters.
**Bloom color/season:** Yellow, cream. Late spring–early autumn.
**Plant hardiness:** Zones 8–10 as perennial; 3–7 as annual.
**Soil needs:** Well-drained. Fertility: Average. 7.0 pH.
**Planting:** Full sun. 1 ft. (30 cm) apart.
**Care:** Easy. Drought-tolerant. Pinch back for bushiness. Propagate by seed, stem cuttings.
**Features:** Good choice for accent, borders, massing in cottage, coastal gardens. Unusual foliage lends interesting contrast to mixed borders. Use to frame garden accessories.

**Common name:** Flax
**Scientific name:** *Linum perenne*
**Description/habit:** Erect, branching, herbaceous perennial, up to 2 ft. (60 cm) tall. Narrow, gray green leaves to 1 in. (25 mm) long; lower plant usually leafless. Short-lived, profuse flowers, shallow-cupped, 1 in. (25 mm) across in branching clusters.
**Bloom color/season:** Blue, white, pink. Late spring–autumn.
**Plant hardiness:** Zones 5–9.
**Soil needs:** Well-drained, sandy, moist. Fertility: Average. 7.0 pH.
**Planting:** Full sun. 1 ft. (30 cm) apart.
**Care:** Moderate. Cut back after flowering. Propagate by seed, cuttings.
**Features:** Good choice for borders in cottage gardens. Will self-sow. Flowers close in shade or late afternoon.

**Common name:** Foxglove
**Scientific name:** *Digitalis* species

**Description/habit:** About 19 species of upright perennials or biennials, 2–3 ft. (60–90 cm) tall. Large, gray green, hairy leaves at base of plant. Flowers bell-shaped with spotted throats, 2–3 in. (50–75 mm) long, hang down on tall showy spikes.
**Bloom color/season:** Pink, purple, yellow, white. Spring–midsummer.
**Plant hardiness:** Zones 3–8.
**Soil needs:** Well-drained, moist. Fertility: Average. 7.0 pH.
**Planting:** Partial shade. 15–18 in. (38–45 cm) apart.
**Care:** Easy. Water moderately. Deadhead to encourage flowering. Crown rot, root rot susceptible. Propagate by division, seed.
**Features:** Good choice for back of mixed borders in cottage, woodland gardens. Attracts bees, butterflies, hummingbirds. May self-sow.

> **Warning**
>
> Foxglove can cause irregular heartbeat if ingested. Avoid planting in gardens frequented by children or pets.

**Common name:** Indigo, False; Wild Blue Indigo
**Scientific name:** *Baptisia australis*

**Description/habit:** Upright, clumping perennial, 2–6 ft. (60–180 cm) tall. Oval blue green leaves, 2½ in. (63 mm) long. Flowers pealike, 1 in. (25 mm), in long terminal racemes.
**Bloom color/season:** Blue. Early summer.
**Plant hardiness:** Zones 3–9.
**Soil needs:** Well-drained. Fertility: Average to poor. 6.5–7.0 pH.
**Planting:** Full sun to partial shade. 18–24 in. (45–60 cm) apart.
**Care:** Easy. Drought-tolerant. Deep rooted. Stake in windy areas. Propagate by division, seed.
**Features:** Good choice for backgrounds, borders, massing, screen in cottage, meadow gardens. Forms very large, mounded clumps of foliage and flowers, to 6 ft. (1.8 m) wide. Good cut flower. Deer-resistant. Eastern U.S. native.

**Common name:** Iris, Siberian
**Scientific name:** *Iris sibirica*

**Description/habit:** Clumping rhizomatous perennial, flower stems to 4 ft. (1.2 m) tall. Grasslike leaves, 1–3 ft. (30–90 cm) long. Flowers showy, long-lasting, 2–5 per plant, upright petals, drooping beardless falls.
**Bloom color/season:** White, blue, yellow, purple. Spring.
**Plant hardiness:** Zones 3–8.
**Soil needs:** Well-drained, moist. Fertility: Average. 6.5–7.0 pH.
**Planting:** Full sun to partial shade. 1–2 ft. (30–60 cm) apart, 1–2 in. (25–50 mm) deep. Plant in autumn.
**Care:** Easy. Water regularly in drought conditions, otherwise moderately. Divide clumps when hollow centers show. Propagate by division of rhizomes.
**Features:** Good choice for accents, borders, massing in cottage, meadow, wetland gardens. Good cut flower. Hundreds of cultivars available.

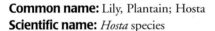

**Common name:** Lavender Cotton
**Scientific name:** *Santolina Chamaecyparissus*
**Description/habit:** Mounding evergreen perennial grown mainly for foliage, 18–24 in. (45–60 cm) tall. Woolly, narrow, finely divided, gray leaves. Flowers button-shaped ½ in. (13 mm) on long stalks.
**Bloom color/season:** Yellow. Summer–autumn.
**Plant hardiness:** Zones 7–10.
**Soil needs:** Well drained; does well on rocky slopes. Fertility: Poor to average. 7.0 pH.
**Planting:** Full sun. 3 ft. (90 cm) apart.
**Care:** Easy. Drought-tolerant. Gets woody, prune rigorously after flowering. Looks best if kept low. Propagate by cuttings.
**Features:** Good choice for borders, edgings, ground cover on banks in cottage, coastal, desert gardens. Deer-resistant. Fire-retardant.

**Common name:** Lily, Plantain; Hosta
**Scientific name:** *Hosta* species
**Description/habit:** As many as 40 species of clumping, spreading perennials. Varieties available from 6–60 in. (15–150 cm) wide. Grown mostly for bold, sumptuous foliage that can be narrow or heart-shaped; wavy- or smooth-margined; quilted, shiny, or velvety; blue green, yellow green, clear green, with yellow, white, or silver markings. Flowers trumpet-shaped, hang down on thin spikes above foliage.
**Bloom color/season:** White, lilac, purple. Midsummer–autumn.
**Plant hardiness:** Zones 3–10.
**Soil needs:** Well-drained, moist. Fertility: Poor to rich. 7.0 pH.
**Planting:** Partial to full shade. 10–30 in. (25–75 cm) apart, depending on species.
**Care:** Very easy. Water in drought conditions. Snail, slug susceptible. Propagate by division.
**Features:** Good choice for borders, ground cover in cottage, woodland gardens. Use along the garden floor and paths to accent other plants.

**Common name:** Lobster-claw; False Bird-of-Paradise
**Scientific name:** *Heliconia* species
**Description/habit:** More than 20 species of tropical evergreen perennials, 6–20 ft. (1.8–6 m) tall. Grown for interesting foliage. Spoon-shaped, medium to dark green leaves, 3 ft. (90 cm) long and wide. Flowers in erect or hanging clusters, 6 in. (15 cm) long. Terminal bloom resembles a lobster claw.
**Bloom color/season:** Green yellow, white, red, with brightly colored bracts. Spring–summer.
**Plant hardiness:** Zones 10–11.
**Soil needs:** Well-drained, moist loam. Fertility: Rich. 6.5 pH.
**Planting:** Partial shade. Space according to desired effect. Attains large size.
**Care:** Moderate. Water regularly. Protect from wind. Propagate by division.
**Features:** Good choice for accent, borders, containers in greenhouses, tropical gardens. Good cut flower. Year-round interest. Tropical Central and South American native.

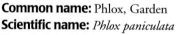

**Common name:** Lupine, Wild
**Scientific name:** *Lupinus perennis*
**Description/habit:** Upright, herbaceous perennial, to 2 ft. (60 cm) tall. Medium green leaves divided into leaflets about 2 in. (50 mm) long. Flowers pealike in dense spikes up to 18 in. (45 cm) long.
**Bloom color/season:** Blue, pink, white. Late spring.
**Plant hardiness:** Zones 4–9.
**Soil needs:** Well-drained, sandy, moist. Fertility: Poor to average. 6.5–7.0 pH.
**Planting:** Full sun to partial shade. 18 in. (45 cm) apart. Score and soak seeds. Sow directly into garden soil.
**Care:** Easy. Water regularly in drought conditions, otherwise moderately. Propagate by division, seed.
**Features:** Good choice for borders in woodland gardens. Eastern U.S. native.

**Common name:** Phlox, Garden
**Scientific name:** *Phlox paniculata*
**Description/habit:** Herbaceous, clumping perennial, with many cultivars; 1–4 ft. (30–120 cm) tall. Oval, narrow leaves, 6 in. (15 cm) long. Fragrant flowers about 1 in. (25 mm) across, in loose oval clusters up to 1 ft. (30 cm) in diameter.
**Bloom color/season:** Red, magenta, pink, purple, white; some with contrasting eye. Summer–autumn.
**Plant hardiness:** Zones 4–8.
**Soil needs:** Well-drained, moist. Fertility: Average to rich. 7.0 pH.
**Planting:** Full sun to partial shade. 18 in. (45 cm) apart.
**Care:** Easy. Water regularly in drought conditions, otherwise moderately. Deadhead to encourage flowering. Powdery mildew susceptible. Propagate by division, seed. Divide every 3–4 years to maintain vigor.
**Features:** Good choice for borders in cottage, meadow gardens. Good cut flower. North American native.

**Common name:** Queen-of-the-Prairie
**Scientific name:** *Filipendula rubra*
**Description/habit:** Clump-forming herbaceous perennial, up to 7 ft. (2.1 m) tall. Leaves large, lobed, mid-green, on branching stems. Flowers numerous, small, with conspicuous stamens, borne in delicate plumes rising like crests of foam above lush, leafy foliage.
**Bloom color/season:** Deep pink. Mid- to late summer.
**Plant hardiness:** Zones 3–9.
**Soil needs:** Well-drained, moist. Fertility: Rich. 7.0 pH.
**Planting:** Full sun to partial shade. 18–24 in. (45–60 cm) apart.
**Care:** Easy. Water during drought conditions. Divide to control spread. Propagate by division, seed.
**Features:** Good choice for borders, massing in cottage, meadow gardens. Use to frame garden accessories. Beautiful and long-lasting cut flower. Popular cultivar is *F. rubra* 'Venusta'. Midwestern U.S. native.

**Common name:** Spurge
**Scientific name:** *Euphorbia* species

**Description/habit:** More than 1600 species of herbaceous perennials, shrubs, and trees. Tiny flowers are surrounded by showy, domed bract. Oblong, medium-textured dark green leaves, turn dark red in autumn.
**Bloom color/season:** Yellow. Spring.
**Plant hardiness:** Zones 5–9.
**Soil needs:** Well-drained. Fertility: Poor to average. 6.0–7.0 pH.
**Planting:** Full sun to partial shade. 12–15 in. (30–40 cm) apart.
**Care:** Easy. Water moderately. Propagate by seed, division in spring or autumn, cuttings.
**Features:** Succulent species are good choice for accents, borders in coastal gardens.

**Common name:** Vervain, Creeping; Rose Verbena
**Scientific name:** *Verbena canadensis*
**Description/habit:** Herbaceous half-hardy perennial, grown as annual in cold climates, to 18 in. (45 cm) tall. Airy see-through appearance. Elliptical, feathery, dark green leaves, 2 in. (50 mm) long. Fragrant flowers, primroselike, in terminal clusters.
**Bloom color/season:** Blue, pink, violet. Summer–autumn.
**Plant hardiness:** Zones 7–10 as perennial; 3–6 as annual.
**Soil needs:** Well-drained soil. Fertility: Average to moderately rich. 7.0 pH.
**Planting:** Full sun, needs heat. 2 ft. (60 cm) apart.
**Care:** Easy. Water infrequently; drought-tolerant. Slug, aphid susceptible. Propagate by seed, cuttings.
**Features:** Good choice for banks, ground cover, walls in cottage, coastal gardens. Fast growing. Deer-resistant. Eastern U.S. native.

**Common name:** Violet, Sweet; English Violet; Florist's Violet
**Scientific name:** *Viola odorata*
**Description/habit:** Many cultivars of clumping perennials, spreading by runners, 4–8 in. (10–20 cm) tall, 12 in. (30 cm) wide. Heart-shaped, toothed, dark green leaves. Fragrant flowers, about 1 in. (25 mm) across, with short spurs on long stems.
**Bloom color/season:** Purple, rarely pink or white. Late winter–midspring.
**Plant hardiness:** Zones 5–9 as perennial; 3–4 as annual.
**Soil needs:** Well-drained, moist. Fertility: Rich, add organic matter. 7.0 pH.
**Planting:** Partial to full shade. 8–12 in. (20–30 cm) apart.
**Care:** Moderate. Water to keep soil moist. Deadhead to encourage flowering. Propagate from seed, runners.
**Features:** Good choice for borders, containers in woodland gardens. Fragrant around entrances. Classic, romantic flower of old-fashioned love stories and films. Invasive in mild-winter climates.

**Common name:** Wake-robin; Trillium
**Scientific name:** *Trillium* species
**Description/habit:** About 30 species of low, lumping perennials of lily family, 6–24 in. (15–60 cm) tall. Long, pointed, oval, 2–6 in. (50–150 mm) leaves in a whorl of 3 at top of stem. One flower rises from center of leaves, 3 petals; 3 in. (75 mm) wide.
**Bloom color/season:** Green to greenish white aging to rose, deep maroon. Spring.
**Plant hardiness:** Zone 3–9.
**Soil needs:** Well-drained, moist. Fertility: Rich. 6.5–7.0 pH.
**Planting:** Partial to full shade. 5–8 in. (12–20 cm) apart.
**Care:** Easy. Best left alone. Propagate by division, seed.
**Features:** Good choice in woodland gardens. Will self-sow. North American native.

**Common name:** Windflower; Anemone
**Scientific name:** *Anemone* species

**Warning**

All parts of windflowers cause hazard of digestive upset or poisoning if ingested. Avoid planting in gardens frequented by children and pets.

**Description/habit:** About 120 species of high-elevation, bushy herbaceous perennials, to 6 ft. (1.8 m) tall. Large, dark green leaves with 3–7 lobes, mostly at bottom of plant. Single flowers, 2–3 in. (50–75 mm) across, in open clusters 1 or 2 ft. (30–60 cm) above leaves.
**Bloom color/season:** Deep pink. Summer–autumn.
**Plant hardiness:** Zones 3–8.
**Soil needs:** Well-drained, sandy loam. Fertility: Average to rich. 7.0 pH.
**Planting:** Full sun to partial shade. 2 ft. (60 cm) apart.
**Care:** Easy. Water regularly in dry weather, otherwise moderately. Caterpillar, aphid susceptible. Propagate by division, seed.
**Features:** Good choice for borders, ground covers in cottage, woodland gardens. Good cut flower. Northern temperate zone native.

**Common name:** Yarrow
**Scientific name:** *Achillea* species
**Description/habit:** Between 60 and 100 species and varieties of upright, clumping perennials, herbaceous or evergreen, 4–60 in. (10–150 cm) tall. Fernlike, spicy-smelling, deep green or gray green leaves, some species with toothed edges. Flowers small, daisylike, borne in broad, flat clusters above foliage; in some species flowers are globular or can be up to 2 in. (50 mm) across.
**Bloom color/season:** White, yellow, rose. Summer–autumn.
**Plant hardiness:** Zones 3–10.
**Soil needs:** Well-drained. Fertility: Poor to average. 7.0 pH.
**Planting:** Full sun. 10–48 in. (25–120 cm) apart, depending on species requirement.
**Care:** Very easy. Water infrequently. Divide every 3–4 years in spring. Propagate by division.
**Features:** Good choice for borders in cottage, meadow gardens. Good cut flower. Deer-resistant. Worldwide distribution.

## BULBS

**Common name:** Bluebell; Wood Hyacinth
**Scientific name:** *Endymion* species
**Description/habit:** Three species of true lily bulbs, to 20 in. (50 cm) tall. Narrow leaves to 2 ft. (60 cm) long, 1½ in. (38 mm) wide. Profuse, fragrant flowers, bell-shaped, ¾ in. (19 mm) long, in erect racemes.
**Bloom color/season:** Blue, white, pink, rose. Spring.
**Plant hardiness:** Zones 4–9.
**Soil needs:** Well-drained, moist. Fertility: Rich. 7.0 pH.
**Planting:** Partial shade. 4–6 in. (10–15 cm) apart, 3–5 in. (75–120 mm) deep.
**Care:** Moderate. Allow to dry in summer. Propagate by offsets.
**Features:** Good choice for drifts under trees, among shrubs in cottage, woodland gardens. Will naturalize. Best if left undisturbed. Good cut flower. Deer- and rodent-resistant.

**Common name:** Crocus
**Scientific name:** *Crocus* species
**Description/habit:** About 75 species of small, Iris family corms, 3–6 in. (75–150 mm) tall. Grasslike, medium green leaves. Flowers cup-shaped on long tubes, appearing stemless; 1½–3 in. (38–75 mm) long; some are fragrant.
**Bloom color/season:** Yellow, lavender, white, purple. Late winter, early spring. Some species are autumn bloomers.
**Plant hardiness:** Zones 3–9; best in cold-winter areas.
**Soil needs:** Well-drained. Fertility: Average. 7.0 pH.
**Planting:** Partial shade. 2–3 in. (50–75 mm) apart, 3–5 in. (75–120 mm) deep.
**Care:** Easy. Protect from rodents. Plant in autumn. Propagate by division.
**Features:** Good choice for borders, edgings, massing in cottage, meadow, woodland gardens. Foliage and flowers are very attractive peeking out from late-season snow.

**Common name:** Crocus, Autumn; Meadow Saffron
**Scientific name:** *Colchicum autumnale*

**Warning**

All parts of autumn crocus are hazardous if ingested. Avoid planting in gardens frequented by children or pets.

**Description/habit:** Deciduous corm of the Lily family, 4–12 in. (10–30 cm) tall. Straplike, floppy leaves 6–12 in. (15–30 cm) long. Flowers long-tubed, flaring, up to 2 in. (50 mm) across, rise from bare earth without foliage.
**Bloom color/season:** Lavender, pink, white. Late summer–early autumn.
**Plant hardiness:** Zones 4–9.
**Soil needs:** Well-drained. Fertility: Average. 7.0 pH.
**Planting:** Full sun. 6–8 in. (15–20 cm) apart, 3–4 in. (75–100 mm) deep. Plant in summer.
**Care:** Easy. Water regularly in dry weather until foliage dies back. Propagate by division.
**Features:** Good choice for borders, containers in woodland gardens. Place where foliage can mature fully. Naturalizes in cold-winter areas. Deer- and rodent-resistant.

**Common name:** Daffodil
**Scientific name:** *Narcissus* species
**Description/habit:** About 25 species, many hybrids, varieties of true bulb. Pale to dark green, flat, straplike leaves. Single or clustered flowers, petals surrounding a trumpet-shaped structure, which can be long or short, smooth or ruffled. Some scented.
**Bloom color/season:** Yellow, white, orange, red, pink, cream, bicolors. Late winter–early spring.
**Plant hardiness:** Zones 3–9.
**Soil needs:** Well-drained, moist. Fertility: Average to rich. 7.0 pH.
**Planting:** Full sun to partial shade. 6–8 in. (15–20 cm) apart, 4–6 in. (10–15 cm) deep. Plant in autumn.
**Care:** Easy. Keep moist during growth, bloom. Propagate by division.
**Features:** Good choice for borders, containers, drifts, massing in cottage, woodland, meadow gardens. Good cut flower. Good for naturalizing under deciduous trees, among shrubs.

**Common name:** Iris, Blue Flag; Wild Iris
**Scientific name:** *Iris versicolor*
**Description/habit:** Fibrous rhizome. Narrow, swordlike leaves 1–4 ft. (30–120 cm) long, upright or recurved. Showy, long-lasting flowers, with upright petals, drooping beardless falls.
**Bloom color/season:** Typically violet blue; other colors are available. Summer.
**Plant hardiness:** Zones 3–8.
**Soil needs:** Very moist soil, water up to 6 in. (15 cm) deep. Fertility: Rich. 6.5 pH.
**Planting:** Full sun. 1–2 ft. (30–60 cm) apart. Plant in autumn.
**Care:** Easy. Keep wet. Propagate by division.
**Features:** Good choice for colorful spring and summer plantings in wetland gardens. Use to frame garden accessories. North American native.

**Common name:** Lily-of-the-Valley
**Scientific name:** *Convallaria majalis*
**Description/habit:** Clumping rhizome, 6–8 in. (15–20 cm) tall. Broad, basal dark green or striped light green leaves, to 9 in. (23 cm) long. Fragrant flowers are small, nodding, bell-shaped, 10–20 per stem.
**Bloom color/season:** White, pink. Spring.
**Plant hardiness:** Zones 2–7. Best in cold-winter climates.
**Soil needs:** Well-drained, moist. Fertility: Average to rich. 7.0 pH.
**Planting:** Partial to full shade. Single pips 4–6 in. (10–15 cm) apart; clumps 1–2 ft. (30–60 cm) apart, 1½–3 in. (38–75 mm) deep. Plant in autumn or early spring.
**Care:** Moderate. Water regularly in dry weather, otherwise moderately. Propagate by division.

**Warning**

All parts of lily-of-the-valley are hazardous if ingested. Avoid planting in gardens frequented by children or pets.

**Features:** Good choice for moist-soil ground cover in cottage, woodland gardens. Good cut flower. Deer- and rodent-resistant. European native naturalized in North America.

# LILY

The sensuous, sumptuous stars of cottage gardens, formal floral arrangements, and medieval religious paintings, these showy flowers can be found along mountain trails and country roadsides as well as in beautifully kept gardens. Over 1,000 species, as well as innumerable hybrids of *Lilium*, provide many lovely options for borders, accents, and for planting in containers.

Erect, unbranched growth and compact whorls of dark green, linear leaves add a bold vertical element to garden design. The flowers may be shaped like trumpets, shallow bowls, funnels, or cups, as many as 20 or 30 on one stem. Their petals curve back gracefully to reveal large red, brown, or golden anthers loaded with pollen on long green filaments. In some species, the petals are recurved to form exotic, dangling shapes often called Turk's caps.

Colors run the range of whites, yellows, and pinks, with bands, stripes, and speckles adding to their allure. Some lilies are only slightly fragrant; others give off an unforgettable perfume. Flowering time is late spring continuing through early autumn.

Plant most lilies in the autumn; in zones 9 and 10, place the bulbs in the vegetable keeper of a refrigerator for 4–6 weeks prior to planting. Put them in the ground about 6–12 in. (15–30 cm) apart, 5–8 in. (13–20 cm) deep, depending on the species. The soil must be well-drained, deep, and loose. Supplement it with organic matter, if needed.

Lilies thrive when their tops are in the sun and their roots are cool and shaded by a ground cover or bushy perennials. Cut off spent blooms, leaving as much of the stem as possible—the stem and leaves are gathering energy for the bulb to use next year.

Popular Asiatic hybrids bloom in early summer, their open flowers facing up, down, or outward. Highly fragrant Oriental hybrids produce huge bowl-shaped blossoms up to 1 ft. (30 cm) across in late summer.

Force lilies by refrigerating their bulbs, then placing them in a shallow dish filled with pebbles or marbles, completely covering the bulb. Water, then place in a warm, well-lit location.

**Common name:** Lily

**Scientific name:** *Lilium* species

**Description/habit:** Between 80 and 90 species of upright true bulbs, 2–6 ft. (60–180 cm) tall. Lance-shaped, shiny, bright green leaves, about 9 in. (23 cm) long. Fragrant flowers trumpet-shaped, 4–5 in. (10–13 cm) across.

**Bloom color/season:** White, yellow, orange, red, purple. Summer.

**Plant hardiness:** Zones 2–9.

**Soil needs:** Well-drained, loose, moist, deep. Fertility: Rich. 7.0–7.5 pH.

**Planting:** Tops in sun, roots in shade. 6–12 in. (15–30 cm) apart. Plant in late summer or early autumn.

**Care:** Easy. Water regularly. Deadhead to remove seedpods. Protect from rodents. Lily mosaic virus susceptible; choose resistant varieties. Propagate by division in autumn.

**Features:** Good choice for stately landscape plants in borders, containers in cottage gardens. Good cut flower. May be forced. Cultivated for more than 2,000 years.

**Common name:** Onion, Ornamental; Allium
**Scientific name:** *Allium* species
**Description/habit:** Over 400 species of true bulbs of the Lily family, 6–60 in. (15–150 cm) tall. Some have broad, flat, others narrow, gray green leaves, 6–12 in. (15–30 cm) long. Flowers small, bell- or star-shaped, in compact or loose clusters on tall, leafless stem, size depending on species; some are fragrant.
**Bloom color/season:** White, pink, violet, red, blue, yellow. Spring–summer.
**Plant hardiness:** Zones 3–10, depending on species.
**Soil needs:** Well-drained, sandy, deep. Fertility: Average. 7.0 pH.
**Planting:** Full sun to partial shade. 4–12 in. (10–30 cm) depending on species. Plant 3 times as deep as bulb is tall. Plant in autumn.
**Care:** Easy. Avoid watering after bloom. Propagate by division, seed.
**Features:** Good choice for accents, borders, containers in cottage, woodland, meadow gardens. Many species, including *A. moly,* naturalize well. Tall species such as *A. giganteum* are great vertical accents. Deer- and rodent-resistant. Northern Hemisphere native.

**Common name:** Sorrel, Wood
**Scientific name:** *Oxalis* species
**Description/habit:** About 850 species of annuals and perennials. Tufted, compact or spreading tuber, rhizome, or true bulb; 4–20 in. (10–50 cm) tall. Green or gray leaves. Flowers 5-petaled, funnel-shaped, 1 in. (25 mm) wide.
**Bloom color/season:** Pink, white, yellow, rose. Spring–autumn.
**Plant hardiness:** Zones 6–9.
**Soil needs:** Well-drained. Fertility: Average to rich. 7.0 pH.
**Planting:** Full sun to partial shade. 6 in. (15 cm) apart, 1 in. (25 mm) deep. Plant in late summer or autumn.
**Care:** Easy. Water in drought conditions. Propagate by division, seed.
**Features:** Good choice for woodland gardens. Deer- and rodent-resistant. Invasive. *O. regnellii* 'Triangularis' has burgundy leaves. Worldwide distribution.

**Common name:** Tulip
**Scientific name:** *Tulipa* species
**Description/habit:** Between 50 and 150 species, hybrids, cultivars of bulbous perennial herbs. Light to dark green, sometimes striped or mottled, straplike leaves. Flowers round, egg-shaped with rounded or pointed petals; single, double, fringed to 4 in. (10 cm) across; closed on gray days; some are fragrant.
**Bloom color/season:** White, cream, yellow, red, pink, orange, purple, maroon, near-black; variegated. Spring.
**Plant hardiness:** Zones 3–10.
**Soil needs:** Well-drained soil. Fertility: Average to rich. 7.0 pH.
**Planting:** Partial shade. 4–8 in. (10–20 cm) apart, depending on species. Plant 3 times as deep as bulb is wide. Plant in autumn.
**Care:** Easy. Allow foliage to fully mature. Propagate by division.
**Features:** Good choice for borders, containers, massing in cottage gardens. Good cut flower. Some species, especially *T. clusiana, T. tarda,* and *T. turkestanica,* naturalize well.

## SHRUBS

**Common name:** Adam's-needle
**Scientific name:** *Yucca filamentosa*
**Description/habit:** Upright, evergreen shrub, 3–5 ft. (90–150 cm) tall. Succulent, swordlike, gray green leaves, some varieties have gold edges, 2 ft. (60 cm) long, 1 in. (25 mm) wide. Fragrant flowers bell-shaped, waxy, drooping, 2–3 in. (50–75 mm) across, on upright stalks 3–5 ft. (90–150 cm) tall.
**Bloom color/season:** White. Midsummer.
**Plant hardiness:** Zones 5–9.
**Soil needs:** Well-drained, sandy. Fertility: Average. 7.0 pH.
**Planting:** Full sun. 4 ft. (1.2 m) apart.
**Care:** Easy. Needs dry soil in winter. Propagate by division, seed, cuttings.
**Features:** Good choice for accent in cottage, coastal, desert gardens. Contributes a sharp, vertical geometry. Use to frame garden accessories. Southeastern U.S. native.

**Common name:** Agave; Century Plant
**Scientific name:** *Agave* species
**Description/habit:** Over 300 species of succulent, rosette-forming shrubs, to 5 ft. (1.5 m) tall, 1–5 ft. (30–150 cm) wide. Strap-shaped, blue green, gray green, dark green, white- or yellow-striped leaves, some with spines, some hooked, 4–72 in. (10–180 cm) long. Flowers small, clustered on long spikes 5–40 ft. (1.5–12 m) tall.

> **Warning**
>
> Sap of agave may cause skin and eye irritation in sensitive individuals.

**Bloom color/season:** Yellowish green. Infrequent.
**Plant hardiness:** Zones 8–10, in areas of low humidity.
**Soil needs:** Well-drained, sandy; tolerates poor soil conditions. Fertility: Average. 7.0 pH.
**Planting:** Full sun, with partial shade in hottest part of the day. Plant from 1–5 ft. (30–150 cm) apart depending on species and effect desired.
**Care:** Easy. Water infrequently. Protect from frost, hot sun.
**Features:** Good choice for accent, containers in coastal, desert gardens.

**Common name:** Azalea
**Scientific name:** *Rhododendron* species
**Description/habit:** Perhaps 800 species, cultivars of deciduous, spreading shrubs, 3–10 ft. (90–300 cm) tall. Oval, bright green leaves, excellent autumn color. Fragrant flowers about 2 in. (50 mm) across.
**Bloom color/season:** Yellow, cream, orange red, pinkish white. Spring–summer.
**Plant hardiness:** Zones 4–9.
**Soil needs:** Well-drained, moist. Fertility: Rich. 6.5 pH.
**Planting:** Full sun; partial shade in hot regions. 4 ft. (1.2 m) apart.
**Care:** Avoid cultivating around plants. Propagate by layering, cuttings.
**Features:** Good choice in woodland gardens. North American native.

**Common name:** Butterfly Bush
**Scientific name:** *Buddleia* species
**Description/habit:** More than 100 species and cultivars of willowlike deciduous or semievergreen shrubs, 3–12 ft. (90–360 cm) tall. Small to large, hairy or felted, gray green to dark green leaves; dark above, light underneath. Fragrant flowers, small, borne in masses of small clusters at end of arching branches.
**Bloom color/season:** Violet, lilac, fuchsia, yellow, white. Spring–summer.
**Plant hardiness:** Zones 5–10.
**Soil needs:** Well-drained, tolerates dry soils. Fertility: Average to poor. 7.0 pH.
**Planting:** Full sun to partial shade. 3 ft. (90 cm) apart.
**Care:** Easy. Deadhead after bloom.In cold-winter climates, prune to the ground in spring; in mild-winter climates, prune about one-third of branches to the ground. Recovers quickly; blooms on new growth. Propagate by seed, cuttings.
**Features:** Good choice for backgrounds, borders in cottage, arid, tropical, gardens. Attracts bees, butterflies, hummingbirds. *B. davidii* is the most common species. Deer-resistant. Worldwide tropical distribution.

**Common name:** Crape Myrtle
**Scientific name:** *Lagerstroemia indica*
**Description/habit:** Deciduous, showy shrub, 5–30 ft (1.5–9 m) tall. Also available as standards. Oblong, dark green, glossy leaves, light green tinged with red or bronze in spring, red or yellow in autumn, 1–2 in. (25–50 mm) long. Flowers crinkled or ruffled, 1½ in. (38 mm) long, in masses of round clusters 6–12 in. (15–30 cm) long.
**Bloom color/season:** Red, rose, pink, purple, white. Summer–autumn.
**Plant hardiness:** Zones 7–10.
**Soil needs:** Well-drained. Fertility: Average. 7.0 pH.
**Planting:** Full sun. 5–30 ft. (1.5–9 m) apart, depending on variety.
**Care:** Easy. Water infrequently and deeply. Prune when dormant. Susceptible to mildew in cool coastal regions. Propagate by seed, cuttings.
**Features:** Good choice for accent in cottage, coastal gardens. Deer-resistant. Fast growing.

**Common name:** Bird-of-paradise
**Scientific name:** *Strelitzia reginae*
**Description/habit:** Trunkless, clumping, evergreen, tropical perennial, 3–4 ft. (90–120 cm) tall. Green to purple-edged, bractlike leaves 18–20 in. (45–50 cm) long, resemble banana leaves. Exotic orange and yellow flowers with dark blue tongue, to 8 in. (20 cm) long, resemble bird in flight.
**Bloom color/season:** Orange, yellow, white, blue blend. Year-round.
**Plant hardiness:** Zones 10–11.
**Soil needs:** Well-drained, moist. Fertility: Rich. 6.5 pH.
**Planting:** Full sun. 3–5 ft. (90–150 cm) apart.
**Care:** Moderate. Water regularly. Protect from wind. Propagate by suckers, division, seed.
**Features:** Good choice for accent, back of borders in tropical gardens. Use to frame garden accessories.

**Common name:** Heavenly Bamboo
**Scientific name:** *Nandina domestica*
**Description/habit:** Evergreen shrub, 30–96 in. (75–240 cm) tall, 2–4 ft. (60–120 cm) wide; dwarf varieties can be as small as 1 ft. (30 cm) tall and 1 ft. (30 cm) wide. Delicate, fine-textured, light green, in some varieties bronze or yellow, bamboolike leaves, 2 in. (50 mm) long. Flowers small, lacy, in loose clusters 6–12 in. (15–30 cm) wide.
**Bloom color/season:** White. Late spring–summer.
**Plant hardiness:** Zones 6–10.
**Soil needs:** Well-drained, moist. Fertility: Average to rich. 6.5–7.0 pH.
**Planting:** Full sun to partial shade. 2–6 ft. (60–180 cm) apart.
**Care:** Easy. Drought-tolerant. Prune canes for bushy growth. Propagate by seed.
**Features:** Good choice for containers, screen. Red berries are more abundant if plants are grouped. Provides autumn, winter color. Deer-resistant.

**Common name:** Hibiscus, Chinese; Hawaiian Hibiscus
**Scientific name:** *Hibiscus rosa-sinensis*
**Description/habit:** Evergreen shrub, 4–15 ft. (1.2–4.5 m) tall. May be dense or open, upright or bushy, depending on variety. Oval, glossy leaves up to 6 in. (15 cm) across. Showy single or double flowers funnel-shaped, 4–8 in. (10–20 cm) wide, some last only a day.
**Bloom color/season:** White, pink, red, yellow, orange. Summer.
**Plant hardiness:** Zones 9–11.
**Soil needs:** Well-drained. moist. Fertility: Rich. 7.0–7.5 pH.
**Planting:** Full sun to partial shade. Space according to desired effect.
**Care:** Moderate. Water deeply, regularly. Deadhead to encourage flowering. Protect from wind, frost. Aphid susceptible. Propagate by layering, cuttings.
**Features:** Good choice for accent, containers, screen, walls in cottage, tropical gardens.

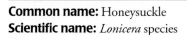

**Common name:** Honeysuckle
**Scientific name:** *Lonicera* species
**Description/habit:** More than 150 species, cultivars of upright or climbing, deciduous or evergreen shrubs, 3–30 ft. (90–900 cm) tall. Oval, green or blue green leaves, 1–6 in. (25–150 mm) long; some species have bronze winter foliage. Flowers 2-lipped, tubular, ½ in. (13 mm) across, ½–2 in. (13–50 mm) long, filled with sweet nectar; some species are fragrant. Black or purple red berries.
**Bloom color/season:** White, coral, pink, yellow. Spring–frost.
**Plant hardiness:** Zones 4–9.
**Soil needs:** Well-drained. Fertility: Average to rich. 7.0 pH; some species do better in either acid or alkaline soil.
**Planting:** Full sun to partial shade. Space according to desired effect.
**Care:** Easy. Some species drought-tolerant. Blooms best with moisture. Aphid susceptible. Propagate by seed, layering, cuttings.
**Features:** Good choice for fences, ground cover, hedge, trellises, walls in cottage gardens. Attracts bees, hummingbirds. Some very invasive. Worldwide distribution.

**Common name:** Lavender, English
**Scientific name:** *Lavandula angustifolia*
**Description/habit:** Compact, bushy, evergreen shrub, 2–3 ft. (60–90 cm) tall, 3–4 ft. (90–120 cm) wide; dwarf varieties 8–24 in. (20–60 cm) tall. Narrow, aromatic, gray green leaves, to 2 in. (50 mm) long. Fragrant flowers, ½ in. (13 mm) long, on 1–2 ft. (30–60 cm) spikes.
**Bloom color/season:** Lavender. Summer.
**Plant hardiness:** Zones 5–10.
**Soil needs:** Well-drained, light, loose soil. Fertility: Average. 7.0–7.5 pH.
**Planting:** Full sun. 18–36 in. (45–90 cm) apart.
**Care:** Easy. Drought-tolerant. Deadhead. Propagate by seed, cuttings.
**Features:** Good choice for borders, edgings, hedges, massing in cottage, western coastal gardens. Good cut or dried flower. Oil of lavender is distilled from this plant. Attracts bees.

**Common name:** Lilac, Common
**Scientific name:** *Syringa vulgaris*
**Description/habit:** Many named cultivars of deciduous, perennial shrub or small tree, 5–20 ft. (1.5–6.0 m) tall and wide. Pointed, oval, dark green leaves 5 in. (13 cm) long. Fragrant flowers small, in large clusters up to 10 in. (25 cm) long.
**Bloom color/season:** Lavender, purple, white, pink. Spring.
**Plant hardiness:** Zones 3–7.
**Soil needs:** Well-drained. moist. Fertility: Rich. 7.5 pH.
**Planting:** Full sun to partial shade in hot regions. 5 ft. (1.5 m) apart. Plant in spring or autumn.
**Care:** Moderate. Water regularly during growth, bloom. Deadhead after bloom. Needs winter chill to bloom well; some varieties have been developed for warmer climates. Powdery mildew susceptible. Propagate by cuttings.
**Features:** Good choice for borders in cottage gardens. Good cut flower. Attracts butterflies. Deer-resistant. Requires 2–3 years to bloom well.

**Common name:** Oleander, Common
**Scientific name:** *Nerium oleander*
**Description/habit:** Bushy, evergreen shrub, 3–20 ft. (90–600 cm) tall, 5–12 ft. (1.5–3.6 m) wide. Narrow, leathery, dark green leaves, 4–12 in. (10–30 cm) long. Double or single flowers, 2–3 in. (50–75 mm) across; some are fragrant.
**Bloom color/season:** White, yellow, red, pink. Spring–autumn.
**Plant hardiness:** Zones 8–11.
**Soil needs:** Moist. Fertility: Average to poor. 7.0 pH.
**Planting:** Full sun. 5 ft. (1.5 m) apart.
**Care:** Easy. Drought-tolerant. Aphid, scale susceptible. Propagate by cuttings.
**Features:** Good choice for borders, containers, hedges, screen along driveways. Best in heat. So tough, used as freeway planting. Attractive all seasons. Fire-retardant. Deer-resistant.

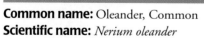

**Warning**

All parts of oleander are fatally poisonous if ingested or smoke is inhaled when plants are burned. Avoid planting in gardens frequented by children or pets.

**Common name:** Oregon Grape; Holly Grape
**Scientific name:** *Mahonia aquifolium*
**Description/habit:** Upright, evergreen, spreading shrub, 3–6 ft. (90–180 cm) tall. Sharp, hollylike leaves in pairs of 5–9 leaflets, 4–10 in. (10–25 cm) long; colors change with season and maturity. Flowers in clusters 2–3 in. (50–75 mm) long. Dark purple berries resemble grapes.
**Bloom color/season:** Yellow. Spring.
**Plant hardiness:** Zones 5–8.
**Soil needs:** Well-drained, moist. Fertility: Average. 7.0 pH.
**Planting:** Partial shade. 3 ft. (90 cm) apart.
**Care:** Easy. Drought-tolerant. Protect from wind. Prune in winter. Propagate by seed, layering, cuttings.
**Features:** Good choice for containers, massing, screen in cottage, woodland gardens. Attracts birds, butterflies. Deer-resistant. North American native.

> **Warning**
>
> All parts of Oregon grape are poisonous if ingested. Avoid planting in gardens frequented by children or pets.

**Common name:** Prickly Pear
**Scientific name:** *Opuntia* species
**Description/habit:** About 300 species of cactus 4–18 ft. (1.2–5.4 m) wide and tall. White or pale gray, broad, flattened joints called pads; spines 1½ in. (38 mm) long. Showy flowers, 3 in. (75 mm) across, along edges of pads. Red or yellow fruits.
**Bloom color/season:** Yellow, sometimes orange, purple. Spring–summer.
**Plant hardiness:** Zones 4–10, if protected.
**Soil needs:** Well-drained. Fertility: Average to poor. 6.5–7.0 pH.
**Planting:** Full sun. Space according to desired effect.
**Care:** Easy. Water during drought conditions, especially during flowering. Protect in cold winter areas. Propagate by seed detaching and rooting pads.
**Features:** Good choice for accents in desert, arid gardens. Place in less-traveled areas because of spiny margins on the pads. Many North American natives.

**Common name:** Sumac
**Scientific name:** *Rhus* species
**Description/habit:** About 150 species of upright, spreading, mostly deciduous shrubs or small trees, 3–20 ft. (90–600 cm) tall. Leathery, deep green leaves divided into leaflets, 2–5 in. (50–125 mm) long; brilliant red or orange in autumn. Flowers in clusters 1–2½ in. (25–63 mm) long. Red, yellow fruit.
**Bloom color/season:** Yellow, white. Early spring–midsummer.
**Plant hardiness:** Zones 3–9.
**Soil needs:** Well-drained, dry, rocky. Fertility: Average to poor. 7.0 pH.
**Planting:** Full sun to partial shade. 3–15 ft. (90–450 cm) apart.
**Care:** Easy. Drought-tolerant. Propagate by seed, layering, cuttings.
**Features:** Good choice for erosion control, ground cover, hedge, screen, walls in woodland, coastal gardens. Some species are fragrant. Many North American natives.

> **Warning**
>
> Three sumac species, poison ivy, sumac, and oak, cause severe contact dermatitis. Avoid planting these in gardens.

**Common name:** Ti Plant; Good-luck Plant
**Scientific name:** *Cordyline terminalis*
**Description/habit:** Many named varieties of palmlike, evergreen shrubs, 6–8 ft. (1.8–2.4 m) tall. Grown for foliage. Leathery, swordlike, deep green, red, pink, or variegated leaves, 4 in. (10 cm) wide, to 3 ft. (90 cm) long. Inconspicuous, scented flowers, in clusters 1 ft. (30 cm) long. Bright red berries.
**Bloom color/season:** White, pink. Summer–winter.
**Plant hardiness:** Zones 10–11. Can be grown in other zones in containers if protected in winter.
**Soil needs:** Sandy, moist, warm. Fertility: Rich. 7.0 pH.
**Planting:** Full sun to partial shade. Space according to desired effect.
**Care:** Easy. Water regularly. Protect from frost. Propagate by layering, cuttings.
**Features:** Good choice for accent, borders, containers in tropical gardens. Often grown indoors. Started from "logs" imported from Hawaii. Sometimes mislabeled as *Dracaena*.

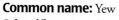

**Common name:** Viburnum; Arrowwood
**Scientific name:** *Viburnum* species
**Description/habit:** More than 225 extremely variable species of upright, bushy, spreading shrubs, 6–15 ft. (1.8–4.5 m) tall; 3½–14 ft. (1–4.2 m) wide. Round or oval, dark green leaves, 3–5 in. (75–125 mm) long; red or bronze in autumn. Flowers variable, in snowballs, lace caps, or flat clusters. Blue, red fruit.
**Bloom color/season:** White, pink, red. Spring–winter.
**Plant hardiness:** Zones 3–9.
**Soil needs:** Well-drained, moist, can tolerate clay. Fertility: Average. 7.0 pH.
**Planting:** Full sun to partial shade. 3–5 ft. (90–150 cm) apart, depending on species.
**Care:** Easy. Generally drought-tolerant. Aphid, mildew susceptible. Propagate by seed, cuttings.
**Features:** Good choice for screen in cottage, woodland gardens. Attracts bees, birds, butterflies. Deer-resistant. Many North American natives.

**Common name:** Yew
**Scientific name:** *Taxus* species
**Description/habit:** Eight species of coniferous evergreen shrubs or trees, to 4–60 ft. (1.2–18 m) tall. Dark green needles, 1 in. (25 mm) long.
**Bloom color/season:** None. Small red berries borne by female plants.
**Plant hardiness:** Zones 3–6.
**Soil needs:** Well-drained. Fertility: Average. 7.0 pH.
**Planting:** Full sun to full shade. Space plantings to avoid pruning.
**Care:** Easy. Water infrequently. Propagate by cuttings.
**Features:** Good choice for hedges, screen in cottage, woodland gardens. Slow growing. Long lived. Northern Hemisphere native.

**Warning**

Foliage and berries of yew are poisonous if ingested. Avoid planting in gardens frequented by children or pets.

## TREES

**Common name:** Birch

**Scientific name:** *Betula* species

**Description/habit:** About 60 species of deciduous trees and shrubs, sometimes multitrunked, 30–100 ft. (9–30 m) tall. Small, pointed, finely toothed leaves. Peeling bark gray, brown, white, pink. Inconspicuous flowers.

**Bloom color/season:** Green leaves, spring; yellow leaves, autumn.

**Plant hardiness:** Zones 2–9, depending on species.

**Soil needs:** Well-drained, moist. Fertility: Average to rich. 6.5 pH.

**Planting:** Full sun. Minimum 4 ft. (1.2 m) apart.

**Care:** Easy. Some species are drought-tolerant. Leaf miner, borer susceptible. Propagate by seed, layering, cuttings.

**Features:** Good choice for accent, borders in cottage, woodland, meadow gardens. River birch, *B. nigra*, an eastern U.S. native, grows 50–90 ft. (15–27 m) tall; leaves 1–3 in. (25–75 mm) long, green above, silvery below; very fast grower at first; trunk forks near ground. Northern Hemisphere native.

**Common name:** Crabapple

**Scientific name:** *Malus* species

**Description/habit:** About 25 species, many varieties of rounded, deciduous trees 15–25 ft. (4.5–7.5 m) tall. Pointed, oval, fuzzy, deep green to purple leaves. Profuse, fragrant flowers 1 in. (25 mm) across. Small red or orange fruits summer–autumn.

**Bloom color/season:** Pink, white. Midspring.

**Plant hardiness:** Zones 3–8.

**Soil needs:** Well-drained. Fertility: Average. 6.5–7.5 pH.

**Planting:** Full sun. Space according to desired effect.

**Care:** Easy. Water in drought conditions. Choose disease-resistant varieties. Propagate by seed, budding.

**Features:** Good choice for accent, back of borders, containers, fences, screen in cottage gardens. Northern Hemisphere native.

**Common name:** Dogwood

**Scientific name:** *Cornus* species

**Description/habit:** About 45 species of horizontally branching deciduous trees, 10–60 ft. (3–18 m) tall. Oval, dark green leaves, 3–5 in. (75–125 mm) long, turn red in autumn. Small flowers in clusters surrounded by 4 showy bracts. Red or blue black berries.

**Bloom color/season:** White, greenish white, yellow. Spring.

**Plant hardiness:** Zones 4–8.

**Soil needs:** Well-drained, moist. Fertility: Average to rich. 6.5 pH.

**Planting:** Full sun to partial shade. Space according to desired effect.

**Care:** Easy. Water regularly. Propagate by cuttings.

**Features:** Good choice for accent, back of borders in cottage, woodland gardens. Fruit attracts birds. *C. florida*, an eastern U.S. native, grows to 20 ft. (6 m). *C. nutallii*, from western U.S. and Canada, grows to 50 ft. (15 m) tall.

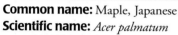

**Common name:** Holly, American
**Scientific name:** *Ilex opaca*
**Description/habit:** Thousands of cultivars of evergreen trees, pyramidal to round-headed, 8–15 ft. (2.4–4.5 m) tall, old trees can be to 50 ft. (15 m). Dull or glossy green leaves with spiny margins, 2–4 in. (50–100 mm) long. Requires both male and female trees to bear fruit.
**Bloom color/season:** Red, yellow berries on female trees. Winter.
**Plant hardiness:** Zones 5–9.
**Soil needs:** Well-drained, moist. Fertility: Rich. 6.5 pH.
**Planting:** Full sun to partial shade. Space according to desired effect.
**Care:** Easy. Water regularly in dry weather, otherwise moderately. Protect from wind. Mulch around plant. Note: both male and female trees required for fruit to set. Propagate by cuttings, grafting.
**Features:** Good choice for background, barrier in cottage gardens. Cut for holiday arrangements. Berries attract birds. Slow growing. North American native.

**Common name:** Maple, Japanese
**Scientific name:** *Acer palmatum*
**Description/habit:** Deciduous tree or shrub, 20–50 ft. (6–15 m) tall. Light green, toothed leaves, deeply cut into 5–9 lobes, 2–4 in. (50–100 mm) long; spring growth is red, turning scarlet or yellow in autumn. Flowers inconspicuous. Spectacularly beautiful branching habit.
**Bloom color/season:** Reddish purple, yellow green, variegated. Late winter –early spring.
**Plant hardiness:** Zones 6–10.
**Soil needs:** Well-drained, moist. Fertility: Average to rich. 6.5 pH.
**Planting:** Full sun to partial shade. Space according to desired effect.
**Care:** Moderate. Water deeply, moderately. Protect from wind. Avoid salt buildup in soil.
**Features:** Good choice for accent, along walls, containers in cottage, woodland gardens. Provides year-round interest.

**Common name:** Pine
**Scientific name:** *Pinus* species
**Description/habit:** About 90 species, named varieties of evergreen, coniferous trees 10 to over 100 ft. (3–30 m) tall. Long, slender needles in bundles of 2, 3, 5, vary in length. Cones vary in shape, 3–6 in. (75–150 mm) long.
**Bloom color/season:** None. Evergreen.
**Plant hardiness:** Zones 3–9.
**Soil needs:** Well-drained. Fertility: Poor to average. 7.0 pH.
**Planting:** Full sun. Space according to desired effect.
**Care:** Easy. Water infrequently. Prune to control shape. Propagate from seed.
**Features:** Good choice for accent, screen in cottage, woodland gardens. Smaller species in containers. Eastern white pine, *P. strobus*, grows to 120 ft. (36 m) tall with blue green needles 4–6 in. (10–15 cm) long, cones 4–6 in. (10–15 cm) long. Western white pine, *P. monticola*, grows 90 ft. (27 m) tall in a narrow, symmetrical habit with blue green needles to 4 in. (10 cm) long, cones 5–8 in. (13–20 cm) long. Dwarf varieties available. Worldwide distribution.

**Common name:** Redbud
**Scientific name:** *Cercis* species
**Description/habit:** Seven species of multitrunked, deciduous shrubs or small trees, 15–35 ft. (4.5–11 m) tall. Broad, rounded, dull green or blue green leaves, turn yellow or red in autumn. Flowers sweet pea-shaped, in clusters, usually appearing profusely before foliage. Smooth, gray bark. Magenta seed pods in autumn.
**Bloom color/season:** Pink, mauve, white. Early spring.
**Plant hardiness:** Zones 4–9.
**Soil needs:** Well-drained, sandy, moist, deep. Fertility: Rich. 7.0 pH; will tolerate acid or alkaline soil.
**Planting:** Full sun to partial shade. Space according to desired effect.
**Care:** Moderate. Water regularly in dry weather, otherwise moderately.
**Features:** Good choice for back of borders in cottage, woodland gardens. Flowers are more profuse in regions of colder winters. Eastern redbud, *C. canadensis*, grows to 35 ft. (11 m) tall. Western redbud, *C. occidentalis*, grows to 15 ft. (4.5 m) tall.

**Common name:** Silver-bell Tree; Wild Olive
**Scientific name:** *Halesia carolina*
**Description/habit:** Ornamental tree with white, bell-shaped flowers ¾ (18 mm) long. Tree grows 15–40 ft. (4.5–12.2 m) tall and (4.5–6 m) wide. Leaves are 2–4 in. (5–10 cm) long and turn yellow in autumn.
**Bloom color/season:** White-pink blend. Spring.
**Plant hardiness:** Zones 5–11.
**Soil needs:** Moist, well-drained soil. Fertility: Rich, acid. 5.0–6.0 pH; Supplement with peat moss or leaf mold.
**Planting:** Light to partial shade. Space 15–20 ft. (4.5–6 m) apart.
**Care:** Easy. Nearly maintenance free.
**Features:** Good choice for spring flower accent and attractive addition near azaleas or rhododendrons. Leaves generally are pest resistant. North American native.

**Common name:** Sweet-gum, American
**Scientific name:** *Liquidambar styraciflua*
**Description/habit:** Narrow, symmetrical, deciduous tree, to over 100 ft. (30 m) tall, 40–50 ft. (12–15 m) wide. Maplelike, finely toothed, glossy, deep green, yellow, purple leaves 4–7 in. (10–18 cm) wide. Inconspicuous flowers. Bark furrowed. Fruits are spiny balls.
**Bloom color/season:** Pale. Spring.
**Plant hardiness:** Zones 5–9.
**Soil needs:** Well-drained, moist, clay and loam. Fertility: Rich. 6.5 pH.
**Planting:** Full sun. Space according to desired effect.
**Care:** Easy. Transplant in spring.
**Features:** Good choice for accent. Slow to establish. Fruits can be messy. Usually grown for superb autumn color, lasting up to 6 weeks. North American native.

## GRASSES

**Common name:** Chinese Grass; Fountain Grass
**Scientific name:** *Pennisetum alopecuroides*
**Description/habit:** Herbaceous perennial mounding grass, 2–4 ft. (60–120 cm) tall, 3–4 ft. (90–120 cm) wide. Bright green leaves, 12–20 in. (30–50 cm) long, turn yellow in autumn. Tiny flowers occur in furry, arching plumes, 4 in. (10 cm) long.
**Bloom color/season:** Pinkish, white, purple. Early summer–autumn.
**Plant hardiness:** Zones 5–9. Does best in warm climates.
**Soil needs:** Well-drained, moist. Fertility: Average. 6.5 pH.
**Planting:** Full sun to partial shade. 1–3 ft. (30–90 cm) apart.
**Care:** Easy. Water sparingly. Protect from wind. Cut back in late winter. Propagate from seed.
**Features:** Good choice for accent, borders, containers, fences, screen, walls in cottage, meadow gardens. Seed heads provide early winter interest. Good in dried arrangements.

**Common name:** Feather Reed Grass
**Scientific name:** *Calamagrosis* × *acutiflora* 'Karl Foerster'
**Description/habit:** Perennial clumping grass, 4–7 ft. (1.2–2.1 m) tall, 6–12 in. (15–30 cm) wide. Arching, bright green leaves, 12–18 in. (30–45 cm) long. Tiny flowers in long, narrow, feathery, upright plumes.
**Bloom color/season:** Green to purplish, aging golden. Early spring–autumn.
**Plant hardiness:** Zones 4–9.
**Soil needs:** Well-drained, moist. Fertility: Average. 7.0 pH.
**Planting:** Full sun to partial shade. 1–2 ft. (30–60 cm) apart.
**Care:** Easy. Water moderately. Cut back in early spring. Propagate by seed.
**Features:** Good choice for accent, screen in cottage, meadow, wetland gardens. Grows best in cool climates. Use to provide windbreak for more delicate companion plantings.

**Common name:** Fescue, Blue
**Scientific name:** *Festuca ovina* var. *glauca*
**Description/habit:** Perennial, tufted grass, 4–18 in. (10–45 cm) tall, 6–8 in. (15–20 cm) wide. Needlelike, bluish gray leaves. Tiny flowers in delicate panicles above foliage.
**Bloom color/season:** Silver fading to tan. Spring–summer.
**Plant hardiness:** Zones 4–9.
**Soil needs:** Well-drained, sandy, moist. Fertility: Poor to average. 7.0 pH.
**Planting:** Full sun. 6–15 in. (15–38 cm) apart.
**Care:** Easy. Somewhat drought-tolerant. Cut back yearly in late winter. Deadhead after blooming. Propagate by seed.
**Features:** Good choice for accent, borders, edgings, ground cover in cottage, coastal gardens. Plant in odd-numbered groups. Provides year-round interest.

**Common name:** Indian Grass

**Scientific name:** *Sorghastrum avenaceum* (*S. nutans*)

**Description/habit:** Perennial bunch grass, 2–5 ft. (60–150 cm) tall, 1–3 ft. (30–90 cm) wide. Arching leaves, 8–12 in. (20–30 cm) long, ¼–½ in. (6–13 mm) wide, turn yellow, orange in autumn. Tiny flowers borne on long, feathery stalks.

**Bloom color/season:** Golden. Summer–autumn.

**Plant hardiness:** Zones 3–9. Grows best in warm climates.

**Soil needs:** Well-drained, moist. Fertility: Average. 7.0 pH.

**Planting:** Full sun to partial shade. 1–3 ft. (30–90 cm) apart.

**Care:** Easy. Drought-tolerant. Cut back in late winter. Propagate by seed.

**Features:** Good choice for accent, background, borders, massing in meadow gardens. Use to frame for garden accessories. Will self-sow. Provides forage, shelter for birds, wildlife. North American native.

**Common name:** Little Bluestem Grass

**Scientific name:** *Schizachyrium scoparium*

**Description/habit:** Perennial tufted grass, 2–5 ft. (60–150 cm) tall, 6–12 in. (15–30 cm) wide. Blue green leaves, ¼ in. (6 mm) wide, turn red orange in winter. Tiny flowers in clusters 2–3 in. (50–75 mm) long.

**Bloom color/season:** White. Summer–autumn.

**Plant hardiness:** Zones 3–10. Grows best in warm climates.

**Soil needs:** Well-drained, moist to dry. Fertility: Average. 7.0 pH.

**Planting:** Full sun. 1 ft. (30 cm) apart.

**Care:** Easy. Water moderately; spreads more in moist soil. Propagate by seed.

**Features:** Good choice for borders, massing in meadow gardens. Slow growing; allow time to reach mature size. Provides excellent autumn color. Contrast element for flowering plants. Provides forage, shelter for birds, wildlife. North American native.

**Common name:** Pampas Grass

**Scientific name:** *Cortaderia selloana*

**Description/habit:** Perennial mounding grass, with fountainlike appearance, 5–10 ft. (1.5–3 m) tall, 6 ft. (1.8 m) wide. Tough, saw-toothed, variegated leaves, 1 in. (25 mm) wide. Small flowers in plumes on long stalks 1–3 ft. (30–90 cm) above foliage.

**Bloom color/season:** White, pinkish. Late summer–autumn.

**Plant hardiness:** Zones 8–10.

**Soil needs:** Well-drained, moist. Fertility: Rich. 7.0 pH.

**Planting:** Full sun. 4 ft. (1.2 m) apart. Space according to desired effect.

**Care:** Easy. Drought-tolerant. Can take dry to wet conditions. Protect from wind. Cut back every few years to maintain form, promote new growth.

**Features:** Good choice for large and dramatic accent, screen in cottage, coastal gardens. Grown for year-round interest. Good in dried arrangements. Fast growing. *C. selloana* 'Pumila' at 3–5 ft. (90–150m) tall is good choice for small gardens. Difficult to eradicate; its cousin, *C. jubata*, is a seriously invasive weed along the Pacific coast.

**Common name:** Switch-grass
**Scientific name:** *Panicum virgatum*
**Description/habit:** Perennial bunch grass, 4–10 ft. (1.2–3 m) tall, 10–20 in. (25–50 cm) wide. Fine-textured, blue green leaves, 12–18 in. (30–45 cm) long, turn yellow, red orange in autumn. Tiny flowers in tall branching groups.
**Bloom color/season:** Reddish. Late winter–autumn.
**Plant hardiness:** Zones 4–9.
**Soil needs:** Tolerates most. Fertility: Average-rich. 7.0 pH.
**Planting:** Full sun. 2–3 ft. (60–90 cm) apart.
**Care:** Easy. Drought-tolerant. Cut back in late winter. Propagate by seed.
**Features:** Good choice for accent, background, ground cover, screen in cottage, meadow, coastal gardens. Use to frame garden accessories. Good in dried arrangements. North American native.

*I feel every garden should have some element of mystery in its design: whatever the size, it is best if not all visible at once.*

*The largest garden looks smaller if you can see it in one glance.*

*Even in the smallest area it must be possible to plant so that there is some element of surprise: peer behind a shrub or over a low wall to discover some pleasant composition of textured leaves or a plant flowering secretly; turn a corner to be "surprised" by some new color; have your mood changed by stepping out of shadow into sunshine.*

*Gardens should invite exploration with a path that curves out of sight: it may lead to nowhere, but has the effect of making you feel that more is to come.*

PENELOPE HOBHOUSE

**Common name:** Tufted-hair Grass
**Scientific name:** *Deschampsia caespitosa*
**Description/habit:** Perennial tufted grass, 1–4 ft. (30–120 cm) tall, 1–3 ft. (30–90 cm) wide. Arching, medium to dark green leaves, 12–18 in. (30–45 cm) tall. Tiny flowers in airy clusters on arching stems 2–4 ft. (60–120 cm) tall.
**Bloom color/season:** Yellow, gold, bronze. Spring–summer.
**Plant hardiness:** Zones 4–9. Prefers cooler climates.
**Soil needs:** Well-drained, moist; tolerates heavy. Fertility: Rich. 6.5–7.0 pH.
**Planting:** Full sun to full shade, best in partial shade. 2–3 ft. (60–90 cm) apart.
**Care:** Easy. Water regularly in drought conditions, otherwise moderately. Propagate by seed.
**Features:** Good choice for borders, ground cover in cottage, woodland, meadow, wetland gardens. Will self-sow. Northern Hemisphere native.

## VINES

**Common name:** Clematis
**Scientific name:** *Clematis* species

**Description/habit:** Over 200 species of sprawling, deciduous or evergreen perennial vines, up to 20 ft. (6 m) long and wide. Dark green leaves divided into leaflets 2–3 in. (50–75 mm) long. Flowers up to 4 in. (10 cm) wide with showy stamens. Fragrant.
**Bloom color/season:** Blue, purple, white, red. Spring–autumn.
**Plant hardiness:** Zones 4–10, depending on species.
**Soil needs:** Well-drained, moist, loose. Fertility: Moderately rich. 7.5 pH.
**Planting:** Full sun to partial shade. 12–18 in. (30–45 cm) apart.
**Care:** Moderate. Water regularly. Mulch. Provide support. Prune. Aphid, earwig, slug susceptible. Propagate by seed, cuttings.
**Features:** Good choice for containers, fences, trellises, tree trunks, walls in cottage, woodland gardens. Northern Hemisphere native.

> **Warning**
>
> The foliage, flowers, and stems of some clematis are harmful if ingested. Avoid planting in gardens frequented by children or pets.

**Common name:** Hydrangea, Climbing
**Scientific name:** *Hydrangea anomala* subsp. *petiolaris*

**Description/habit:** Sprawling, woody, deciduous vine, to 75 ft. (23 m) in extent. Heart-shaped, dark green leaves, 2–4 in. (50–100 mm) long. Small, fragrant flowers in flat clusters 6–10 in. (15–25 cm) wide. Red, shedding bark.
**Bloom color/season:** White. Summer–autumn.
**Plant hardiness:** Zones 5–10.
**Soil needs:** Well-drained, moist, loose. Fertility: Rich. 6.5–7.0 pH.
**Planting:** Full sun to partial shade. Space according to desired effect.
**Care:** Easy. Water regularly. Prune to control size. Climbs by rootlike holdfasts, can get top heavy; provide support. Propagate by cuttings, layering.
**Features:** Good choice for fences, screen, shade structures, walls in cottage, woodland gardens.

**Common name:** Morning Glory
**Scientific name:** *Ipomoea* species

**Description/habit:** About 500 species of twining, tender perennial vines, 6–12 ft. (1.8–3.6 m) tall, 10–30 ft. (3–9 m) wide. Medium to dark green, heart-shaped or 3-lobed leaves, 3–8 in. (75–200 mm) wide. Single or double, funnel-shaped flowers, 4–6 in. (10–15 cm) wide.
**Bloom color/season:** Red, white, blue, variegated. Summer–autumn.
**Plant hardiness:** Zones 3–10.
**Soil needs:** Well-drained, moist. Fertility: Average to rich. 7.0 pH.
**Planting:** Full sun to partial shade. Space according to desired effect.
**Care:** Easy. Water sparingly. Protect from wind. Soak, scrape, or notch seeds to encourage sprouting. Aphid susceptible. Propagate by scarified seed.
**Features:** Good choice for banks, trellises in cottage, tropical gardens. Most open only in morning. Climbs rapidly. May self-sow. Worldwide distribution.

**Common name:** Philodendron
**Scientific name:** *Philodendron Selloum*
**Description/habit:** Upright, evergreen treelike vine, 2–8 ft. (60–240 cm) tall, 6–8 ft. (1.8–2.4 m) wide. Grown for distinctive foliage. Leathery, glossy, deeply cut, dark green leaves to 3 ft. (90 cm) long. Flowers callalike, about 1 ft. (30 cm) long, with bracts surrounding club-shaped spike.
**Bloom color/season:** White, greenish. Blooms appear only on older plants if heat, light, humidity are right.
**Plant hardiness:** Zones 10–11.
**Soil needs:** Well-drained, loose, moist. Fertility: Rich. 7.0 pH.
**Planting:** Partial shade. 6–8 ft. (1.8–2.4 m) apart.
**Care:** Moderate. Water regularly. Protect from wind, frost. Feed regularly. Provide support. Propagate by seed, cuttings.
**Features:** Good choice for containers, fences, walls in tropical gardens. Fast growing. Grows best where roots are cramped. Often grown indoors.

**Common name:** Trumpet Vine; Trumpet Creeper
**Scientific name:** *Campsis radicans*
**Description/habit:** Deciduous vine, to more than 20 ft. (6 m) in extent. Pinnate leaves with 9–11 toothed leaflets, 2½ in. (63 mm) long. Flowers trumpet-shaped, flaring, 3 in. (75 mm) long, 2 in. (50 mm) across, in large showy clusters. Attractive seed capsules, 5 in. (13 cm) long.
**Bloom color/season:** Orange, scarlet. Summer.
**Plant hardiness:** Zones 5–10.
**Soil needs:** Well-drained, loose soil. Fertility: Average. 7.0 pH.
**Planting:** Full sun to partial shade. Space according to desired effect.
**Care:** Easy. Water moderately. Prune to control growth. Propagate by seed, layering, cuttings.
**Features:** Good choice for accent, fences, trellises, walls in cottage, woodland gardens. Excellent choice for shade structures; stays in full leaf throughout hot summers. Fast growing. Spreads by suckers. North American native.

**Common name:** Virginia Creeper; American Ivy; Five-Leaved; Woodbine
**Scientific name:** *Parthenocissus quinquefolia*
**Description/habit:** Sprawling, deciduous vine of indefinite extent. Leaves in 5 toothed leaflets, bronze in spring, mature to dark green, turn brilliant color in autumn. Inconspicuous flowers. Blue black berries.
**Bloom color/season:** Greenish. Early summer.
**Plant hardiness:** Zones 3–10.
**Soil needs:** Tolerates most. Fertility: Average. 7.0 pH.
**Planting:** Full sun to full shade. 3–4 ft. (90–120 cm) apart.
**Care:** Easy. Water regularly. Japanese beetle susceptible. Propagate by seed, layering, cuttings.
**Features:** Good choice for fences, ground cover, trellises, walls in cottage, woodland, coastal gardens. Excellent choice for year-round interest. Fast growing, limited only by support. Berries attract birds. Eastern U.S. native.

## GROUND COVERS

**Common name:** Bugleweed
**Scientific name:** *Ajuga reptans*
**Description/habit:** Creeping, evergreen ground cover forming thick carpet, 6–10 in. (15–25 cm) deep. Oval leaves can be green, bronzy, variegated with white or rose, 2–4 in. (50–100 mm) wide. Flowers tubular, 2-lipped, on spikes 4–6 in. (10–15 cm) high.
**Bloom color/season:** Deep blue. Late spring–early summer.
**Plant hardiness:** Zones 3–9.
**Soil needs:** Tolerates most. Fertility: Poor to average. 7.0 pH.
**Planting:** Partial to full shade. 6–18 in. (15–45 cm) apart.
**Care:** Easy. Water regularly in dry weather, otherwise moderately. Leaf burn, rot, fungal diseases susceptible. Propagate by division.
**Features:** Good choice for borders in cottage, woodland gardens. Spreads by runners.

**Common name:** Lilyturf, Creeping
**Scientific name:** *Liriope spicata*
**Description/habit:** Clumping, creeping, evergreen herbaceous ground cover, 8–10 in. (20–25 cm) tall. Grasslike, deep green leaves, to 18 in. (45 cm) long. Flowers small, bell-shaped to tubular, in clusters on spikes.
**Bloom color/season:** Lilac, purple, white. Summer–autumn.
**Plant hardiness:** Zones 5–9.
**Soil needs:** Well-drained, sandy. Fertility: Average. 7.0 pH.
**Planting:** Full sun to full shade. 8–15 in. (20–38 cm) apart.
**Care:** Easy. Deadhead to promote additional blooms. Slug, snail susceptible. Propagate by division.
**Features:** Good choice for edging, ground cover in cottage, tropical gardens. Excellent choice for gardens with an Asian theme. Use as garden floor in sunny and shaded spaces.

**Common name:** Mint
**Scientific name:** *Mentha* species
**Description/habit:** About 25 species and many cultivars of creeping, perennial herbaceous ground cover, 1–3 ft. (30–90 cm) tall. Pungent, oval to lance-shaped, toothed or smooth, crinkly or curly, dark green to grayish green leaves, to 2 in. (50 mm) long. Flowers small, tubular, 2-lipped, in spikes.
**Bloom color/season:** Pink, white, purple. Summer–autumn.
**Plant hardiness:** Zones 4–9, depending on species.
**Soil needs:** Tolerates most. Prefers well-drained, sandy, moist. Fertility: Average. 6.5–7.0 pH.
**Planting:** Full sun to partial shade. 3 ft. (90 cm) apart.
**Care:** Easy. Can withstand total neglect. Propagate by division, cuttings.
**Features:** Good choice for containers, ground cover in cottage, coastal gardens. Very invasive. Many culinary, flavoring, and medicinal uses.

**Common name:** Plumbago, Dwarf
**Scientific name:** *Ceratostigma plumbaginoides*
**Description/habit:** Spreading, evergreen ground cover, 6–12 in. (15–30 cm) tall, 15 in. (38 cm) wide. Glossy, bronze green leaves, 3 in. (75 mm) long, turn reddish in autumn. Flowers ½–1 in. (13–25 mm) wide.
**Bloom color/season:** Deep blue. Summer–frost.
**Plant hardiness:** Zones 5–9.
**Soil needs:** Well-drained, loose, sandy. Fertility: Average. 7.0 pH.
**Planting:** Full sun to partial shade. 18 in. (45 cm) apart.
**Care:** Easy. Avoid overwatering. Cut back, mulch in cold-winter climates. Propagate by division and cuttings.
**Features:** Good choice for borders, massing in cottage gardens. Late to leaf in spring, pairs well with early bulbs. Underground stems cover large areas.

**Common name:** Rosemary
**Scientific name:** *Rosmarinus officinalis*
**Description/habit:** Many cultivars of perennial herb grown as ground cover, some erect, some prostrate, 12–16 in. (30–40 cm) tall, to 3 ft. (90 cm) wide. Fragrant, leathery, linear, dark green or gray green leaves. Flowers tubular, 2-lipped, ¼–½ in. (6–13 mm).
**Bloom color/season:** White, pink, lavender, blue. Spring–autumn.
**Plant hardiness:** Zones 7–10.
**Soil needs:** Well-drained, sandy. Fertility: Average to poor. 7.0–7.5 pH.
**Planting:** Full sun. 2 ft. (60 cm) apart.
**Care:** Easy. Drought-tolerant. Prune. Propagate by cuttings.
**Features:** Good choice for banks, borders, containers, hedges, walls in cottage, western coastal gardens. Attracts bees. Deer-resistant. Salt-tolerant. Cultivated since Roman times for culinary and medicinal uses.

**Common name:** Stonecrop
**Scientific name:** *Sedum* species
**Description/habit:** About 600 species and many varieties and cultivars of matting, evergreen, succulent, ground cover, 10–24 in. (25–60 cm) tall, up to 18 in. (45 cm) wide. Fleshy blue green, gray green, purplish leaves. Flowers small, in flat-topped clusters.
**Bloom color/season:** Pink, red, yellow, white. Spring–autumn.
**Plant hardiness:** Zones 3–10.
**Soil needs:** Well-drained. Fertility: Average to poor. 7.0 pH.
**Planting:** Full sun to partial shade. 10–12 in. (25–30 cm) apart.
**Care:** Easy. Limit waterings. Drought-tolerant. Crown or root rot susceptible if overwatered. Propagate by division, offsets, cuttings, seed.
**Features:** Good choice for borders, containers, walls in cottage, meadow, coastal, desert gardens. Some species may be grown indoors. Shape, color of foliage provide interesting contrast. Golden carpet, *S. acre*, which grows 2 in. (50 mm) tall with yellow flowers in spring, is an excellent choice for planting between pavers and stepping stones. Northern Hemisphere native.

**Common name:** Thrift; Sea Pink
**Scientific name:** *Armeria maritima*
**Description/habit:** Widely cultivated, clumping, evergreen, perennial herbaceous ground cover, 6 in. (15 cm) tall, 1 ft. (30 cm) wide. Stiff, grasslike, bright green leaves. Flowers in globular clusters, ¾ in. (19 mm) wide on stems 10–12 in. (25–30 cm) long.
**Bloom color/season:** Pink. Spring–summer.
**Plant hardiness:** Zones 4–10.
**Soil needs:** Well-drained, dry, sandy. Fertility: Average. 7.0 pH.
**Planting:** Full sun. Prefers areas of low heat, low humidity. 1 ft. (30 cm) apart.
**Care:** Easy. Water infrequently. Cut back after bloom. Spreads slowly from season to season. Propagate by seed, cuttings.
**Features:** Good choice for accent, between rocks, borders, containers, edgings in cottage, coastal gardens. Good cut flower. Salt-tolerant. May self-sow. Worldwide distribution.

**Common name:** Thyme
**Scientific name:** *Thymus* species
**Description/habit:** Over 400 species and many named varieties of creeping, matting, or shrubby evergreen ground cover, ½–12 in. (13–300 mm) tall, 8–36 in. (20–90 cm) wide. Fragrant, small, linear or oval, gray green to dark green leaves, can be variegated with gold or white. Flowers small, 2-lipped, on whorled spikes.
**Bloom color/season:** White, magenta, lilac, pink. Summer.
**Plant hardiness:** Zones 4–9.
**Soil needs:** Well-drained. Fertility: Average. 7.0–7.5 pH.
**Planting:** Full sun. 1–2 ft. (30–60 cm) apart, depending on species and desired effect.
**Care:** Easy. Drought-tolerant. Pinch to control shape. Cut back in summer for second growth and bloom. Propagate by division or cuttings.
**Features:** Good choice for between pavers and stepping stones, borders, containers, walls in cottage, coastal gardens. Attracts bees. Many culinary uses; one of the *fines herbes* of French cuisine.

**Common name:** Woodruff, Sweet
**Scientific name:** *Galium odoratum*
**Description/habit:** Creeping, perennial ground cover, 4–10 in. (10–25 cm) tall, with indefinite spread. Leaves linear, whorled, bright green. Fragrant flowers, tiny, star-shaped, in whorled clusters.
**Bloom color/season:** White. Spring–early summer.
**Plant hardiness:** Zones 4–8.
**Soil needs:** Well-drained. Fertility: Rich. 7.0–7.5 pH.
**Planting:** Partial shade. 1 ft. (30 cm) apart.
**Care:** Moderate. Water regularly in dry weather, otherwise moderately. Propagate by division, seed.
**Features:** Good choice for borders in cottage, woodland gardens. Leaves fragrant when dried.

## FERNS

**Common name:** Lady Fern
**Scientific name:** *Athyrium Filix-femina*
**Description/habit:** Many varieties of spreading fern growing from a rhizome; evergreen in mild climates, otherwise deciduous; 1–4 ft. (30–120 cm) tall, 2 ft. (60 cm) wide. Fronds thin, finely divided, light to dark green.
**Bloom color/season:** None. Fiddleheads, or young bracts, appear in spring.
**Plant hardiness:** Zones 3–8.
**Soil needs:** Well-drained, moist. Fertility: Rich. Supplement with organic matter. 6.5–7.0 pH.
**Planting:** Partial to full shade. 2–3 ft. (60–90 cm) apart.
**Care:** Easy. Keep soil constantly moist. Propagate by division, offsets, spores.
**Features:** Good choice for shade areas in cottage, woodland, tropical gardens. Provides textural interest. Plant beside dark tree trunks to reveal fern's foliage. Northern Hemisphere native.

**Common name:** Maidenhair Fern
**Scientific name:** *Adiantum pedatum imbricatum*
**Description/habit:** Herbaceous or evergreen fern, 18–24 in. (45–60 cm) tall, 2 ft. (60 cm) wide. Finely cut, fingerlike, drooping, bright green fronds spread parallel to ground. Stalks black or purple.
**Bloom color/season:** None. Fiddleheads, or young bracts, appear in spring on fibrous, black wirelike stalks.
**Plant hardiness:** Zones 3–8.
**Soil needs:** Well-drained, moist. Fertility: Rich. Supplement with organic matter. 7.5 pH.
**Planting:** Partial to full shade. 9–24 in. (23–60 cm) apart.
**Care:** Moderate. Keep soil moist. Slug susceptible. Propagate by division, offsets, spores.
**Features:** Good choice for containers, shade areas in cottage, woodland gardens. *A. pedatum*, a relative, is known as 'Five-Finger Fern.' Northwestern American native.

**Common name:** Sword Fern, Western
**Scientific name:** *Polystichum munitum*
**Description/habit:** Upright, evergreen fern, vase-shaped, 1–2 ft. (30–60 cm) tall, 2½ ft. (75 cm) wide. Leathery, shiny, dark green fronds. Clumps may have up to 100 fronds.
**Bloom color/season:** None. Fiddleheads, or young bracts, appear in spring.
**Plant hardiness:** Zones 5–9.
**Soil needs:** Well-drained, moist. Fertility: Rich, add organic matter. 6.5 pH.
**Planting:** Partial to full shade. Minimum 3 ft. (90 cm) apart.
**Care:** Easy. Somewhat drought-tolerant.
**Features:** Good choice for accent, ground cover in woodland gardens. Often grown indoors. Good in flower arrangements. Christmas Fern, *P. acrostichoides*, is its eastern relative. North American native.

# USDA Plant Hardiness Around the World
## North America

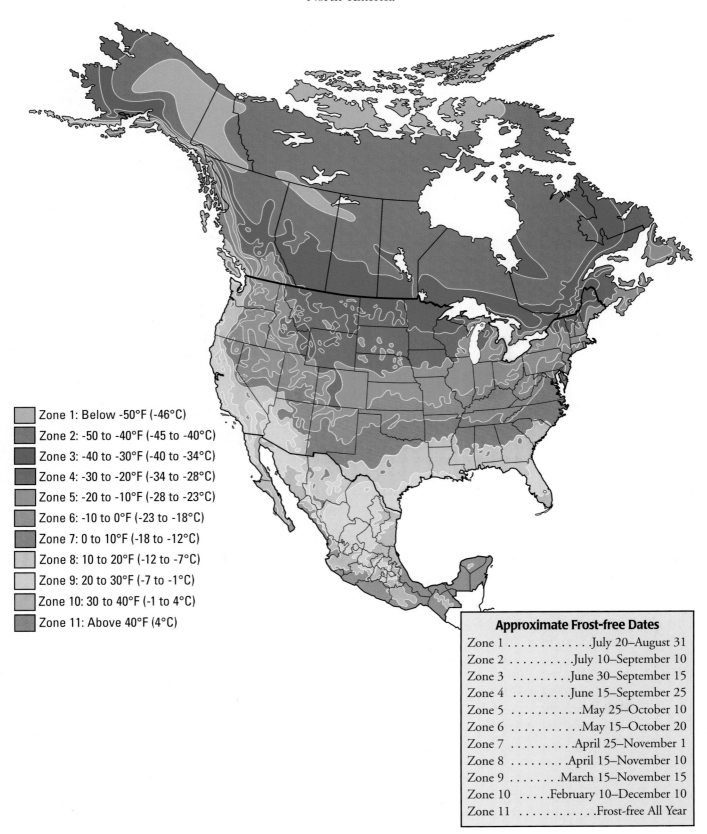

Zone 1: Below -50°F (-46°C)

Zone 2: -50 to -40°F (-45 to -40°C)

Zone 3: -40 to -30°F (-40 to -34°C)

Zone 4: -30 to -20°F (-34 to -28°C)

Zone 5: -20 to -10°F (-28 to -23°C)

Zone 6: -10 to 0°F (-23 to -18°C)

Zone 7: 0 to 10°F (-18 to -12°C)

Zone 8: 10 to 20°F (-12 to -7°C)

Zone 9: 20 to 30°F (-7 to -1°C)

Zone 10: 30 to 40°F (-1 to 4°C)

Zone 11: Above 40°F (4°C)

**Approximate Frost-free Dates**

Zone 1 . . . . . . . . . . . .July 20–August 31

Zone 2 . . . . . . . . .July 10–September 10

Zone 3  . . . . . . . .June 30–September 15

Zone 4  . . . . . . . .June 15–September 25

Zone 5  . . . . . . . . . .May 25–October 10

Zone 6  . . . . . . . . . .May 15–October 20

Zone 7  . . . . . . . . .April 25–November 1

Zone 8  . . . . . . . .April 15–November 10

Zone 9  . . . . . . .March 15–November 15

Zone 10  . . . . .February 10–December 10

Zone 11  . . . . . . . . . . .Frost-free All Year

# USDA Plant Hardiness Around the World
## Australia

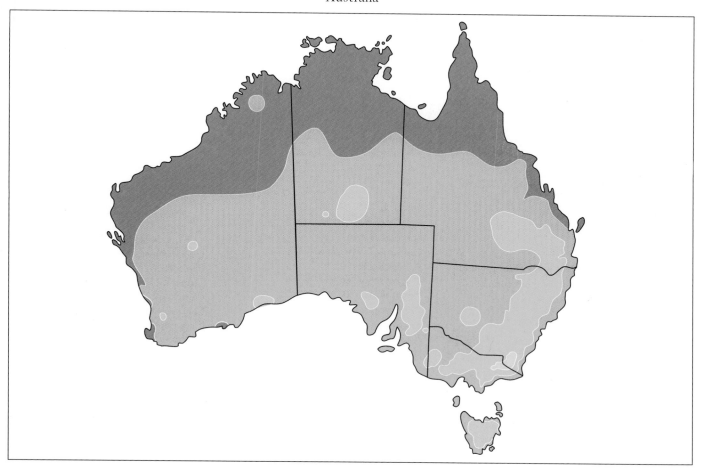

South Africa

New Zealand

Europe

# ON-LINE INDEX

# I N D E X

# I N D E X